D1596898

ARCHITECTURE'S
DESIRE

Writing **Architecture** series

A project of the Anyone Corporation

THE MIT PRESS

CAMBRIDGE, MASSACHUSETTS

LONDON, ENGLAND

ARCHITECTURE'S DESIRE

READING THE LATE AVANT-GARDE

K. MICHAEL HAYS

MIT Press books may be purchased at special quantity
discounts for business or sales promotional use.
For information, please email special_sales@mitpress.mit.edu
or write to Special Sales Department, The MIT Press,
55 Hayward Street, Cambridge, MA 02142.

This book was set in Filosofia by ~~Graphic Composition, Inc.~~
Printed and bound in the United States of America.

Library of Congress Cataloging-in-Publication Data

Hays, K. Michael.
Architecture's desire : reading the late avant-garde /
K. Michael Hays.
p. cm.—(Writing architecture)
Includes bibliographical references.
ISBN 978-0-262-51302-9 (pbk. : alk. paper)
1. Architecture, Modern—20th century—Philosophy. I. Title.
II. Title: Reading the late avant-garde.
NA680.H413 2010
724'.6—dc22
                                                    2009006132

10 9 8 7 6 5 4 3 2 1

CONTENTS

ACKNOWLEDGMENTS

During the years of writing toward the topic of architecture's desire, I presented related work at several schools and had fruitful discussions with many colleagues. I am especially grateful for criticisms and suggestions from the faculty and students of the TU Delft and the Ohio State University. My own students at Harvard have made invaluable contributions to my thinking about this material. And I have especially benefited from sustained discussions with Pier Vittorio Aureli (who also pointed me to the drawing used on the cover), George Baird, Michael Bell, Marco de Michelis, Jeffrey Kipnis, Sanford Kwinter, Mary Lou Lobsinger, John McMorrough, Toshiko Mori, Winifried Elysse Newman, Diana Ramirez, Anthony Vidler, Val Warke, and Jim Williamson. I am deeply thankful to Fredric Jameson for his comments on an early draft.

Portions of some analyses included here have appeared in *Cities of Artificial Excavation: The Work of Peter Eisenman, 1978–1988* (New York: Rizzoli, 1994), *Sanctuaries: The Last Works of John Hejduk* (New York: Whitney Museum and Abrams, 2002), and *Bernard Tschumi* (New York: Rizzoli, 2003). My essay "Prolegomena Linking the Advanced Architecture of the Present to That of the 1970s through Ideologies of Media, the Experience of Cities in Transition, and the Ongoing Effects of Reification," in *Perspecta* 32 (Cambridge: MIT Press, 2001), was proto- to the present proposition.

I thank Matthew Abbate and Margarita Encomienda at the MIT Press for their patience and care with the text and design. Cynthia Davidson nurtured and directed this project at every stage.

ARCHITECTURE'S DESIRE

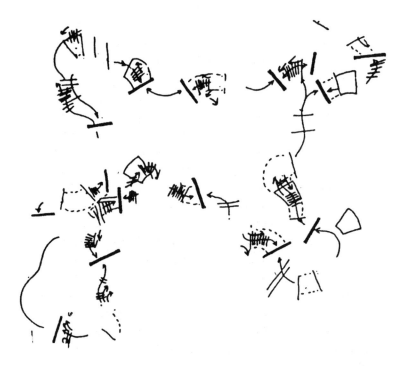

DESIRE

I write here about architecture's status as a domain of cultural representation. I am not primarily concerned with architecture as the art of building per se; nor do I consider it as a profession. Rather, I examine architecture as a way of negotiating the real, by which I mean intervening in the realm of symbols and signifying processes at the limit of the social order itself—that is, architecture as a specific kind of socially symbolic production whose primary task is the construction of concepts and subject positions rather than the making of things. It is thus an architectural impulse or attitude that I seek to characterize, and a certain kind of attention is needed to detect it: specialized theoretical techniques and methods must be brought to bear on this subject. Nevertheless, I hope to suggest too that the architectural impulse is part of daily social life and its wide-ranging practices. Architecture comprises a set of operations that organize formal representations of the real (although I will have to complicate that formulation), and hence, rather than merely being invested with an ideology by its creators or users, it is ideological in its own right—an imaginary "solution" to a real social situation and contradiction (as Louis Althusser's take on Jacques Lacan puts it); that is what is meant by its "autonomy."[1] Understood in this way, architecture's effects—the range of conceptual and practical possibilities it both enables and limits—as well as the irreducible affects it presents are a precious index of the historical and social situation itself. I am concerned here with the effects and affects as well as the facts of architecture.

If ontology is the theory of objects and their relations—a structure within which being itself may be given some organization—then, I believe, art (generally) and architecture (especially) can and do operate ontologically. Architecture is fundamentally an inquiry into what is, what might be, and how the latter can happen. Architecture is one way of attaining the verb "to be." But my problem is not philosophical; rather, it is historical—that is, I want to investigate a moment in history when certain ways of practicing architecture still had philosophical aspirations. The expanded decade of the 1970s (which I will take to include roughly the years between 1966 and 1983) saw a search for the most basic units of architecture and their combinatory logics. Aldo Rossi's singular typological fragments; Peter Eisenman's frames, planes, and grids; John Hejduk's wall and its nomadic adventures; and Bernard Tschumi's cinegrammatic segments, which frame and trigger the architectural impulse itself—all were understood as fundamental architectural entities and events that could not be reduced or translated into other modes of experience or knowledge. This self-consciousness also aimed for an awareness of architecture's position in society and history itself (philosophical thinking always turns historical when pushed to its limits); thus ideological-representational engagements of architecture with the expanding consumer society of the 1970s were probed, and various strategies of distortion, resistance, and reappropriation were devised. The very nature of subject-object constructions and relations and of the subject's relation to its other was opened to a scrutiny as intense as any philosophical inquiry. And architecture reached a limit condition in which its objects were no longer construed as mere elements and assemblages of building, however complicated or sophisticated, but rather as a representational system—a way of perceiving and constructing identities and differences.[2]

Such ontological ambitions were recognized even at the time; they are implicit in the widespread and recurrent analogies between architecture and the ultimate system of self-consciousness that is language. Indeed, another way of characterizing the period in question would be to call it "Architecture in the Age of Discourse," a designation that has the advantage of aligning architecture with other disciplines that similarly turned to language in their own respective self-examinations. As Jacques Derrida put it, "This moment was that in which language invaded the universal problematic; that in which, in the absence of a center or origin, everything became discourse—provided we can agree on this word—that is to say, when everything became a system where the central signified, the original or transcendental signified, is never absolutely present outside a system of differences."[3]

Judgments about the meaning and value of the discursive turn, however, were not all positive. "The return to language is a proof of failure," Manfredo Tafuri declares, and though his position is more ambivalent than this assertion would indicate, he never wavers from his argument that, by the 1970s, what remains of modernity is only a spectral sense of our existence, in which we wrestle with the barely perceptible and unsolid echoes of an architectural past that cannot be recovered and a future that will not arrive. The advanced architecture of the 1970s must therefore remain a "salvage operation" in which "the elements of the modern architectural tradition are all at once reduced to enigmatic fragments—to mute signals of a language whose code has been lost—shoved away haphazardly in the desert of history.[4]

Tafuri's analysis finds architecture in a double bind. To the extent that architecture can function in a capitalist society, it inevitably reproduces the structure of that society in its own immanent logics and forms. When architecture resists, capitalism withdraws it from service—takes it off-line—so that demonstrations by architects of the critical distance of their practice from degraded life become redundant and trivialized in advance. This transmutation of the cold, all-encompassing blueprint of a mode of production into the pure formalization of aesthetic technique is architecture's destiny, its "plan." And having identified that, Tafuri asserts the intolerable but inescapable conditions of possibility for contemporary architecture: to collapse into the very system that condemns architecture to pure means-end instrumentality, or to retreat into hypnotic solitude, recognizing that there is no longer a need for architecture at all. Thus "'the disenchanted avant-garde,' completely absorbed in exploring from the comfort of its charming *boudoirs* the profundities of the philosophy of the unexpected, writes down, over and over again, its own reactions under the influence of drugs prudently administered."[5]

The "over-and-over-again" indictment of the postwar avant-garde—the empty, numbing repetition of forms left over from the presumed-authentic historical avant-garde—became something of a leftist critical trope after Peter Bürger's *Theory of the Avant-Garde* (German, 1974; English, 1984). Bürger's derogatory term *neo-avant-garde* therefore suggests itself as an appropriate appellation for the work I am interested in here. Certainly the repetition of the formal elements and operations of Le Corbusier, de Stijl, and constructivism is the most immediately apparent characteristic of the experiments of Eisenman, Hejduk, and Tschumi, if not Rossi, whom one might nevertheless think of as a neo-Enlightenment-avant-gardiste. Bürger's categorization seems inescapable: "The neo-avant-garde institutionalizes the *avant-garde as art* and thus negates genuinely avant-gardiste intentions. This is true independently of the consciousness artists have of their activity, a consciousness that may perfectly well be avant-gardiste. . . . Neo-avant-gardiste art is autonomous art in the full sense of the term, which means that it negates the avant-gardiste intention of returning art to the praxis of life."[6]

The *neo*-ness of this work is made all the more compelling in the specific medium of architecture by the fact that not only Tafuri but also the more conservative Colin Rowe came to all but the same conclusion earlier and independently of Bürger. According to Rowe, if the historical avant-garde shared common ideological roots with Marxism, it also shared a Marxist philosophical ambition to interfuse form and word—variously articulated as expression and content, system and concept, practice and theory, building and politics, or (in Bürger's terms) art and life. That the fusion ultimately failed may be attributed to a shift in the terms in which the experience of modernity itself had to be conceived in postwar architecture—a shift from modernity fully developed as the essential desired goal of architecture to modernity as architecture's limiting condition. In his introduction to *Five Architects*, Rowe asserts what seems to be the only possible choice for the advanced architecture of the time: adhere to the forms, the *"physique*-flesh" of the avant-garde, and relegate the *"morale*-word" to incantation. For if the latter has been reduced to "a constellation of escapist myths," the *physique* still "possess[es] an eloquence and a flexibility which continues now to be as overwhelming as it was then." The measure of architecture lies no longer in the efficacy with which it prefigures a new and better world but rather in its achievement within the contingent conditions of the modern, of meeting the demands of the flesh, as it were, of elevating form as its own language without reference to external sentiments, rationales, or indeed social visions: "The great merit of what follows lies in the fact that its authors are not enormously self-deluded as to the immediate possibility of any violent or sudden architectural or social mutation." The plastic and spatial inventions of cubism and constructivism, of Giuseppe Terragni, Adolf Loos, Mies van der Rohe, and Le Corbusier, remain the standard specific to the ideologically indifferent medium of architecture itself. The architects of the postwar avant-garde are "belligerently second hand,"

Scamozzis to modernism's Palladio, a series of simulacra. Yet it is only through the acceptance of that standard and the repetition of just those simulacra that architects' aspirations can be intelligible.[7]

This is the story, then, on which Tafuri and Rowe agree: In a first moment, the revolutionary avant-gardes of the early twentieth century surgically probe the modern city itself—the sociopsychological metropolis of Georg Simmel, Georg Lukács, and Walter Benjamin—in order to identify the patterns of its essential characteristics, which can then be converted into artistic form; in Tafuri's words:

> *To use that experience as the foundation for visual codes and codes of action borrowed from already established characteristics of the capitalist metropolis—rapidity of change and organization, simultaneity of communications, accelerated rhythms of use, eclecticism—to reduce the structure of artistic experience to the status of pure object (an obvious metaphor for the object-commodity), to involve the public, as a unified whole, in a declaredly interclass and therefore antibourgeois ideology: such are the tasks taken on, as a whole, by the avant-gardes of the twentieth century.*[8]

In a second moment, a dimension of achieved autonomy of form allows architecture to stand against the very social order with which it is complicit, yet the same complicity racks architecture into an agonistic position—combative, striving to produce effects that are *of* the system yet against it. But the language of forms thus discovered—simple geometrical volumes, serialized points and lines, diagonal vectors, planes in vertical layers and horizontal stacks, frames and grids—takes on an absolute autonomy with the result that, in a final moment, the architectural neo-avant-garde can peel the language off from the real, repeating the same already reified forms but transforming them into a self-enclosed, totally structured system of signs. The repetition of the neo-avant-garde is that "of someone who is aware that he is committing a desperate action whose only justification lies in itself. The words of their vocabulary, gathered from the lunar wasteland remaining after the sudden conflagration of their grand illusions, lie precariously on that slanting surface that separates the world of reality from the solipsism that completely encloses the domain of language."[9] In this view, in the architecture of the age of discourse we witness the "freeing of architectural discourse from all contact with the real."[10]

The lack of a social need for architecture; architecture's total loss of the real: there is plenty of evidence in the works and writings of the architects in question to support Tafuri's conclusion. But a brief excursus will suggest a more dialectical position than either Tafuri or Rowe allows. Rossi and Eisenman, for example, are explicitly and especially sensitive to the effects of reification, but their work is not just a victim of its effects; they critically inscribe these effects. In Rossi's typological thinking, the relentless fragmentation, atomization, and depletion of the architectural elements seem to follow precisely the process that Lukács called reification (*Verdinglichung*). And yet typology (very like the realism recommended by Lukács), involves the power to think generally, to take up the fragments and organize them into groups and to recognize processes, tendencies, and qualities where reification yields only lifeless quantities. What is more, for Lukács the form of experience that most concretely represents the force of reification is crisis—that point where, as in Tafuri's analysis, the mnemonic function of architecture is just about to fail, where the memory banks have become so compartmentalized and arid that they will hold nothing other than the most bleached-out material. At this stage, the cognitive vocation of architecture is to reflect or to cause reflection on the processes behind such crisis: crisis is modulated into critique.

We can begin to restore the social and historical meaning of type making—and indeed of the larger project under consideration that typology helps inaugurate—by positing it as an abstraction from a specific historical moment, a crisis, even a moment of trauma. For the very conditions on which the typology project depends—namely, the continuing tradition of the European city as documented in Rossi's *L'architettura della città* (1966)—had, by the time of this theorization, already disappeared as a contemporaneous object of experience, giving way to the city of information, advertisement, and consumption. By 1971 Denise Scott Brown (just to give one example) had proposed that the communication across space of the social values of groups had superseded the more conventional sorts of need for architecture. "Las Vegas, Los Angeles, Levittown, the swinging singles on the Westheimer Strip, golf resorts, boating communities, Co-op City, the residential backgrounds to soap operas, TV commercials and mass mag ads, billboards, and Route 66 are sources for a changing architectural sensibility," writes Scott Brown. "In fact, space is not the most important constituent of suburban form. Communication across space is more important, and it requires a symbolic and a time element in its descriptive systems."[11]

We need not rehearse the ways in which mass media changed the very nature of the experience of public space during this time, except to recall that advertising media joined with the extensive development of buildings on the outskirts of the city and the new distribution of services to suburban commercial zones, making it more difficult to control the quality of urban space through traditional tectonic and typological means. Message reception challenged the tactile experience of objects, and voice, as it were, became *tenant lieu* of the full body; information now structured space and prepared it for experience. Scott Brown, Robert Venturi, and others seized on the new perceptual conventions adequate for comprehension within this new system. The perception of architectural surfaces began to overtake the experience of urban space in the traditional sense. Image consumption began to replace object production, and the sheer heterogeneity of images exploded any single, stable typology of the city. Public meaning was now to be found in the signs and perceptual habits forged in a pluralist, consumerist, suburban culture. Consequently a split was felt to have opened up between the European tectonic-typological tradition and the everyday world of the American popular environment, a split that was fundamental to theoretical debates of the 1970s.

The point, however, is that none of this was missed by Rossi. For while Rossi's typological obsessions seem to be a way of constantly confirming the determinate presence of the traditional European city—refracting its historical logic of form through a neo-Enlightenment lens in contingent, contradictory, and quasi-surreal ways—their peculiar mnemonic function also makes it possible to see in them a new beauty in precisely that which is vanishing. The originality of Rossi's work may well be its capacity to convey, alternately with melancholy or unblinking disenchantment, that the traditional European city—which in some sense means architecture itself—is forever lost, and that the architectural avant-garde has reached an end. Tafuri insisted as much in a direct response to what Massimo Scolari, speaking of Rossi and the Tendenza, considered a refounding of the discipline: "The thread of Ariadne with which Rossi weaves his typological research does not lead to the 'reestablishment of the discipline,' but rather to its dissolution, thereby confirming *in extremis* the tragic recognition of Georg Simmel and György Lukács: 'a form that preserves and is open to life, does not occur.' In his search for the Being of architecture, Rossi discovers that only the 'limit' of Being there is expressible."[12]

While the work of Rossi and the Tendenza and that of Scott Brown and Venturi make up two more or less divergent problematics, the fact that they are similar even in their differences was recognized in the theoretical literature of the mid to late 1970s. Mario Gandelsonas's dialectical negation of the differences between the "neorationalism" of Rossi and the "neorealism" of Scott Brown and Venturi with his category of "neofunctionalism" is only the first example of a widespread theoretical attempt to resolve the contradictory aspirations of an architectural representation of the sociocultural moment together with an architectural autonomy in the face of the same.[13] What has not been noticed is the fact that Peter Eisenman's "postfunctionalism," formulated in his 1976 editorial response to Gandelsonas and developed in the decade after in his "cities of artificial excavation," is a simultaneous absorption and displacement of the same two problematics (neorationalism and neorealism)—a double negation or neutralization of Gandelsonas's neofunctionalism. But the counterdialectic that Eisenman twists out of this scheme is the position that the autonomy project must be extended because the heterogeneity of the consumerist, mediatic city has now collapsed under its own weight, producing not difference but sameness. For Eisenman, architecture does not so much aspire to autonomy, as with Rossi, as it is *forced* into it by the very system it seeks to represent. The price of autonomy is a reduction in and a specialization of form, which becomes cut off from other social concerns even as, in its very isolation and aridness, it becomes perfectly adequate for, representative of, and homologous with the society that sponsors it. What Venturi and Scott Brown present as the discovery of happily possible, practical futures, Eisenman recognizes as nothing more than a misprojection of our own baleful historical moment and subjective situation.

The interpretations of Tafuri and Rowe encode the premise that the postwar "disenchanted" avant-garde symbolizes the torsions, contradictions, and closures of a certain historical and social moment. This view does not sufficiently recognize, however, the more dialectical fact that this architecture—in its very objectivity and autonomy—has already internalized that with which the critics intend to confront it: that is, architecture has already incorporated the annulment of its own necessity (both its functional and representational vocations) and consequently *recoded* the object as the symbolic realization of just that situation. This architecture is a reflection on the foundations and limits of architecture itself. I shall therefore adopt a different terminology and refer to the architecture and the ethos of this group as the *late* avant-garde, with all the connotations this contradictory locution entails: of intransigence and survival beyond what should have ended; of a moment in a larger trajectory beyond which one cannot go; of technique accumulated to the point of bleak rumination; of productive negativity. In the late phase, the architectural symbolic begins to close in on itself, to regard itself as a vast accumulation of signifiers rather than as the never-concluded, positive production of meaning. The late avant-garde's introjection of loss and absence means not that the architectural object is empty, lacking, freed of contact with the real—as Tafuri and Rowe have it—but rather that the object renders its pathological content directly; it is the very form in which a certain lack assumes existence, the form necessary to imagine a radical lack in the real itself.

The term *late avant-garde* has the advantage of association with Fredric Jameson's *late modern*, by which he intends an extreme reflexivity within the modern itself rather than a replay of modernism—that is, a condition in which the ideology (understood as a positive and necessary framework for practice) of modernism has been theorized and identified in terms of artistic autonomy, "a return to art about art, and art about the creation of art." Unlike the fully commercialized postmodernism, the late architectural avant-garde keeps its namesake's commitment to rigorous formal analysis, making the material of architecture stand against consumerism. But unlike the historical avant-garde, it self-consciously closes in on its own limits rather than opens outward; its original site is one of the trauma of having arrived too late. After all, when everything has been accounted for, how do you account for what remains? The late avant-garde "can never take place in any first time, but is always second when it first happens."[14] The term also recalls Theodor Adorno's concept of "late style" and Edward Said's elaboration of it. Said sees lateness as an unresolved contradiction involving "a nonharmonious, nonserene tension, and above all, a sort of deliberately unproductive productiveness going *against*." It is made possible at certain moments in modern history "when the artist who is fully in command of his medium nevertheless abandons communication with the established social order of which he is a part and achieves a contradictory, alienated relationship with it. His late works constitute a form of exile."[15]

Against the received view of Tafuri and Rowe, the examination of the late avant-garde undertaken in the following chapters shows a different relation between architecture and the real, of architecture's representation of the real. It will become evident that the received view of Tafuri and Rowe is not so much incorrect as it is not correct enough. For the real is not so easily dealt with as the received view implies—it is not just *there* before some material symbolic practice makes it manifest. Architecture's imperative is to grasp something absent, to trace or demarcate a condition that is there only latently. In short, my thesis is that having long since been deprived of its immediate use value, architecture in the 1970s found itself challenged as a mode of cultural representation by more commercially lubricated media. Feeling the force of changed historical conditions and a developed consumer society, the most advanced architecture of the 1970s retracted the frame of identity between the architectural object and the sociomaterial ground (on this, so far, all are in accord). This retraction is a form of pragmatic negation that follows the historical avant-garde's strategies of resistance—a variant demanded by a new situation, but one that produces an impasse, since resistance seems no longer to bring change (and this is where Tafuri leaves it). At this point, however, the most advanced architecture forces a transduction upward, as it were, to a higher plane of abstraction—a transition from the outward-directed negativity of the historical avant-garde (which produced an architectural object that, through certain demystifying operations, strived to resist or disrupt the very situation that brought it into being) to a second-order negativity, an architecture reflecting on Architecture (whose object consequently becomes internally split, as we will see). The architectural object as such is disenfranchised (though not necessarily destroyed), annulled as an immediate thing and reconceived as a mediating material and process. The object-in- itself becomes an object-different-from-itself, a signifier directed toward the very disciplinary codes and conventions that authorize all architectural objects—it becomes Symbolic in Lacan's sense. The object becomes a medium for a Real that it does not simply reproduce, but necessarily both reveals and conceals, manifests and represses.

A certain pattern emerges. What in the received view appears as the conditions of impossibility for an architectural system— a historical and social situation in which there is no need for architecture as a cultural representation or, rather, in which its representational domain has no access to any reality beyond it—in fact establishes the conditions for new and different architectural functions. For as soon as architecture's need is articulated as *symbolic*—as soon as the architectural object is presented anew, repeated as *symbolized*—an inquiry is launched into architecture's possibilities rather than its actualities: Where does architecture come from, and what authorizes its existence as architecture—beyond the particular constitutions already in place? This is the query of the late avant-garde. To which in response they

1.1
Aldo Rossi, *Dieses ist lange her—
ora questo è perduto*, 1975, drawing.
Courtesy Fondazione Aldo Rossi.

Dieses ist lange her / Ora questo è perdu

7/30 AR 75

offer *not architecture itself but evidence that it exists*, as Adorno might say.[16] But the pattern of the response is Lacanian. An empirical need reorganized in a medium of the Symbolic is what Lacan distinguishes as a demand, which directs its signifiers to an Other (originally the Mother, or language itself, but here something exterior to architecture, something beyond its grasp, which I characterize in the chapters that follow) that is experienced as intervening in (granting, denying, limiting) the satisfaction of the need. When need is reorganized as demand, the immediate, actual object of need is sublated (Lacan uses the Hegelian nomenclature of *Aufhebung*) only to reappear in mediated form—as the avatar of a dimension transcendent to the immediate object (the dimension of the Mother's love, in the original instance; a horizon at the limit of architecture in the present instance, architecture's essential but absent structure) and the process-object through which that dimension finds expression.[17]

We are in the matrix of desire (we have been all along). In the Lacanian system, desire is "the force of cohesion which holds the elements of pure singularity together in a coherent set," where "the elements of pure singularity" are understood as nothing less than the most basic signifying units of the unconscious.[18] Which is to say that desire is the machine that runs the entire psychic system. Desire is the constant production, connection, and reconnection of signifiers, of architectural quanta, of the pulsating flows of pure interpretation; this is why Lacan so insistently identifies desire and metonymy. What I suggest here and in the chapters that follow is that architectural desire is materialized in the objects of the late avant-garde—the symbolic desire constituted by architecture's "big Other," its laws and language, its original oneness; desire as the architectural unconscious; desire as the pursuit of architecture's original object forever lost (the Tabernacle in the desert, the Vitruvian tree house, the primitive hut).[19] Hence the obsessive search in this work for architecture's fundamental codes and principles, all the time knowing full well there can be none, that outside the architectural Symbolic is the radical nothingness of the architectural Real. Hence too the tumbling into the abyss as desire seeks its object: for desire desires *itself* in its object. It determines itself by negating its object, then becomes the object abolished through its own self-appropriation. Lacan's formula is, "Desire is the desire for desire, the desire of the Other."[20] And we can feel the full significance of the advent of desire at this particular moment in architecture's history by recognizing that architectural desire arises as a kind of absolute alterity exactly when the possibility of architecture's nonexistence is glimpsed on the horizon. In other words, the question of how architecture exceeds itself is the other side of imagining architecture's end. Thus the late avant-garde is the form architecture assumes when it is threatened with its own dissolution.

The marks of desire are various. They include the reduced, single volumes and fragments that populate Rossi's ghost-lit cityscapes and Hejduk's carnivalesque villages, and the even more minimal el-cubes of Eisenman and cinegrams of Tschumi—all bits and pieces from the architectural Symbolic understood as *analogues* of the social text (which by the 1970s had seen its possibilities similarly reduced and minimized). And the *repetitions* of these same forms are desire looking for its object and constantly missing the mark ("this is not *that*"), an insatiable quest best understood, as we will see, on the model of an architectural death drive. These architects address the matter explicitly: Eisenman, whose "end of the end" seeks to abolish history to fulfill itself; Rossi, with his allegorical drawing of striving *Dieses ist lange her / Ora questo è perduto* (this is long gone: architecture survives because the time of its fulfillment has passed);[21] Hejduk, with his wall event, "which . . . might also be considered the moment of death";[22] and Tschumi, whose Manhattan Transcripts are an entire screenplay of death and desire. Through desire, architecture is rendered eccentric to itself. And there are moments when an architectural experience produces that conception of eccentricity—moments of becoming, affects, *encounters* that are nonrepresentational modes of thought; moments when a sensation just barely precedes its concept and we glimpse very basic, primitive architectural ideas, axioms for future architectures. Encounter and event are particularly operative in the work of Hejduk and Tschumi (Tschumi coined the term *event-space* in architecture), but all of these architects find ways to dislocate architectural experience, opening it up to the

```
3 Masterpieces of late-twentieth-century design theory.


1. Rossi's Inequality, aka the Architectural Memory Theorem
```

$$ \text{[house shape]} > \triangle + \text{[trapezoid]} $$

```
The minimum meaningful architectural configuration is
greater than and irreducible to its geometric constituents.


2. Hejduk's Inequality, aka the Architectural Poetry
Theorem
```

$$ \text{[form]} > \text{[form]} + \text{[form]} $$

```
The minimum poetic architectural configuration is greater
than and irreducible to architectural memories.


3. Eisenman's Hypothesis aka the Architectural Calculus
Theorem
```

$$ (\triangle, \square, \text{[form]}, \text{[form]}, \text{[form]}, \cdots) \subset \left[\langle \diamond \times \langle \right] $$

```
    Minimum geometric, mnemonic and poetic configurations are
special cases of a generalized calculus of form.
```

1.2
Jeffrey Kipnis, *3 Masterpieces of Late-Twentieth-Century Design Theory*, 1990.

fact that all perception is partial and ideological. Their work has been called "critical" in recognition of this characteristic. Yet I believe that the concept of desire more adequately signals their corollary attempt to escape the ideological closures of the situation through the portals of the libidinal and the collective; "critical" implies perhaps a too cerebral asceticism of specialized elites, though that too is correct as far as it goes. Moreover, I am insisting that the work under investigation here does more than extend the compulsory critical negativity of the historical avant-garde. In a theoretical sense, an architecture that, by internalizing critical negativity, posits itself as eccentric to itself is even more radical.

The complete absorption of structuralist tenets into architecture had by the 1970s made it possible to think architectural form as the effect of relations of difference among elements that themselves had no substantive meaning—Ferdinand de Saussure's "difference without positive terms." The late avant-garde, on the other hand, is the exact inversion of that formulation: it presents a singular architecture different from itself—an architecture that, in order to install itself as architecture, must already be marked, traced, transgressed, and divided from itself by memories of a past (Rossi and Hejduk are explicit about this) and anticipations of a future continuing identity (as Eisenman and Tschumi differently insist). I will follow Derrida in using the term *spacing* to refer to this tearing of the singularity from itself, this internalized differing. Therefore, the metonymy of architecture's desire is: *analogy, repetition, encounter, spacing*. Each component will be developed in the readings of architecture that follow.

But for now, we are finally in a position to situate the representational range of late avant-garde architecture from the spatial Imaginary to the codes and laws of the Symbolic in the larger nonrepresentational field of the Real. And it should be made clear now that my understanding of the Real follows the readings of Lacan by scholars like Fredric Jameson and Slavoj Žižek and is best summarized by Jameson's famous pronouncement that the Real "is simply History itself."[23] It is interesting in the present context to remind ourselves that it was Jameson's confrontation with the negative thought of Tafuri that virtually forced the production of Jameson's correlate to the Real-as-History, which is the imaginary projection he calls cognitive mapping. The imperative to think totality is one on which Tafuri and Jameson agree (and dealing with the Real must always involve a totalizing propensity). Yet for Jameson, architecture still has the important social function of articulating material forces that would otherwise remain ungraspable and linking the local, phenomenological, and subject-centered experiences of space to the developing subject-producing structures of capitalism itself. And right where Tafuri sees the fading away of class ("there can never be an aesthetics, art or architecture of class"),[24] Jameson finds the residue of what used to be called class consciousness—a mapping of one's social place—but of a paradoxical kind, premised on the representation of the "properly unrepresentable" global structure in each of the local, experiential moments that are themselves the effects of that structure. Cognitive mapping is fundamentally a development of Althusser's radical rewriting of ideology as "a representation of the imaginary relationship of individuals to their real conditions of existence," itself, of course, a reading of Lacan's Imaginary-Symbolic-Real triad. Cognitive mapping is, on one side, a kind of collective "mirror stage" in which the affective immediacies of identity are in dialectical play with the alienating closures and misrecognitions that are the byproducts of any representation at all. But at the same time, the map is also a trace-trait of the social Symbolic, a "social symbolic *act*" with potential to break out from its ideological prison. Beyond that, at the limit of the Symbolic order, is the Real—"History itself"—which supports the social even as it remains obdurately unavailable and unsymbolizable. "Conceived in this sense," Jameson writes,

History is what hurts, it is what refuses desire and sets inexorable limits to individual as well as collective praxis, which its "ruses" turn into grisly and ironic reversals of their overt intention. But this History can be apprehended only through its effects, and never directly as some reified force. This is indeed the ultimate sense in which History as ground and untranscendable horizon needs no particular theoretical justification: we may be sure that its alienating necessities will not forget us, however much we might prefer to ignore them.[25]

Jameson's History—"absent cause," "unrepresentable" and "unsymbolizable," the "untranscendable horizon," "Necessity"—is always in place but only as an undifferentiated and ultimately intractable outside (Lacan defines the Real as "that which resists symbolization absolutely"): the vanishing point of the Symbolic and Imaginary alike, the end of the line toward which their plays of presence and absence, signifiers and images incline. The late architectural avant-garde is, in the end (at the end), a reckoning with this Real.

Jameson's "History is what hurts" passage was published in 1981. It is interesting to ponder whether it is analytical or symptomatic of its time. In any case, History is what hurt architecture at precisely this same moment, as the practico-inert began to turn back on and against the accumulate practices of architecture. And the sense one has when scanning the fractured landscape of the late avant-garde, of a failure that is alternately inevitable and deliberate, and a finality that is dreaded but enjoyed—these are explainable only as effects of History's contradictions.[26] The architecture of the late avant-garde performs the impossibility of architecture's full realization; it stages an architectural project that for historical reasons must be undertaken but ultimately is brought to failure by a dynamic integral to the project itself. Such are the workings of architecture's desire.[27]

ANALOGY

Mobilized explicitly against the scientism not only of modernist functionalism but also of the remaining positivist design methodologies and operations research of the 1960s, which sought to arrive at optimal architectural organizations mathematically and avoid the slippery problems of architectural representation and translation, *Meaning in Architecture* (1969), edited by Charles Jencks and George Baird, proposed a preliminary semiotics of architecture elaborating the basic structuralist insight that buildings are not simply physical supports but artifacts with meaning—signs dispersed across some larger social text.[1] The repercussions of this and similar structuralizations of architecture as critiques of functionalist and positivist dogmas would prove enormous, extending over the next decade of architecture theory, and the essays in *Meaning in Architecture* are but early examples of what would quickly become a widespread search for a system of architectural meaning.

But if the structuralist projection into architecture was perhaps inevitable (structuralism is designed to manage all cultural systems of signification) and in certain ways already latent in earlier models of architectural interpretation (those of Emil Kaufmann, John Summerson, or Rudolf Wittkower, for example), the most pertinent and fruitful level of homology between architecture and language still had to be decided. In other words, what was to be the scale of architecture's structure? Is an individual work or group of works like a language, or is architecture as a whole structured like a language? The first view has affinities with traditional treatments of buildings as organic units whose origins and intentions of formation must be elucidated, whereas the second view, which the editors of *Meaning in Architecture* adopt and which would become the disciplinary norm, shifts the interpretive vocation considerably. No longer is the interpreter's task to say *what* the individual work means (any more than it is the linguist's task to render the meanings of individual sentences); rather, it is to show *how* the codes and conventions of architecture enable objects to produce meaning. Questions are raised about users' and readers' expectations, about how a structure of rules enters into and directs the design of a work, about how any architectural "utterance" is a shared one, having been spoken already and therefore shot through with qualities and values—questions, in short, about architecture's public, ideological life. Moreover, the goal or limit condition of the theoretical project, in this view, is to analyze not just buildings or projects but the whole of the system of architectural signification.

George Baird's essay from that volume, *"La Dimension Amoureuse* in Architecture," follows Roland Barthes's early semiotics to reveal some basic issues about the structure of architectural signification. First, if architecture as a whole is like a language (a specifically encoded grammar, or *langue*), then the individual work is a particular instantiation or effect of that generalized language (analogous to a speech act, or *parole*)—the architect cannot simply assign or take away meaning, and that meaning cannot be axiomatic.[2] According to this semiotics, architecture is a readable text, and the protocols and parameters of its legibility are what we mean by *rhetoric*. Rhetoric operates within the structure of shared expectations and demands a social, dialogical, even erotic relationship with the reader—Baird's "amorous dimension." But rhetoric is not simply a subjective expression. Its procedures are inseparable from processes of argument and justification with respect to the social function of making architectural sense.

The most productive dimension of Baird's essay (though he does not take full advantage of it) is his setting of Claude Perrault's concepts of positive and arbitrary beauty into active equivalence with the *langue/parole* system. For what is achieved in the complex fraction—positive beauty is to arbitrary beauty as *langue* is to *parole*—should not be understood as a simple simile of architecture as language; nor should it be understood in terms of the more complex assertion that the individual work of architecture must be perceived differentially against the network of the architectural system as a whole. For Perrault's positive beauty is applied not just to *an* architecture (the classical language, say, or some other specific style) but to *all* of architecture—to Architecture. The implication of the complex fraction is that any individual work of architecture, in all its contingency, locality, and arbitrariness, can be dissolved back into a specifically architectural but universal structured system—a symbolic order—of which it is a partial instantiation.

There is one more important corollary of this machinery. Though Baird does not mention it, his semiotic fraction is capable of generating out of its binaries a third term, which might articulate the reciprocal exchanges between the discursive network of architecture as a whole and the individual instances of that system—a kind of synthetic operator between the symbolic system and the specific architectural signifier. The reemergent notion of architectural typology attempts to do just that.[3] The logic of types asserts that the various elements of architecture are not in themselves full of meaning; they are not items that have substantial content. Rather, they are relational forms, elements in a structured system on the same order and of the same relative scale as phonemes in language (or what Claude Lévi-Strauss, in his study of myth, called "mythemes").[4] *Architectemes*, as we might call them, make up the basic mechanism of architectural thought: the distinctive, recurring combinations of such elemental units are types, and the logic of their organization is typology. Few terms from the architecture theory of the late 1960s and early 1970s carry the same power as that of typology, and the reason, I suggest, lies in type's mediating position in architecture's imagination and symbolization.

A passage from Adorno's 1965 reflection on functionalism and architecture will help explain the work of imagination:

> *Architecture inquires: how can a certain purpose become space; through which forms, which materials? All factors relate reciprocally to one another. Architectonic imagination is, according to this conception of it, the ability to articulate space purposefully. It permits purposes to become space. It constructs forms according to purposes. Conversely, space and the sense of space can become more than impoverished purpose only when imagination impregnates them with purposefulness.* Imagination breaks out of the immanent connections of purpose, to which it owes its very existence.[5]

Architectural imagination (*Einbildungskraft*, the work of making images and schemata) exceeds any empirical demand made on architecture with a form and an affective force beyond reason or end, form or function. Consider an example. Let us give the name *place* to the architectural affect of purpose-becoming-form, that is, to a hypothetically originary architectural condition. (At its most primitive level architecture has always been seen as a mimesis and an analogue of natural conditions: the accident of a tree branch falling across two trunks is turned into an entire system of support and measure; the continuation of a ridge line becomes a wall marking the territory of a group; the clearing of a field becomes a city.) Architecture, or the vocation of architecture's imagination, then, is fundamentally the making of a place, where place is understood to have certain formal, dimensional properties—a space marked off as distinct—as well as a specific set of uses or purposes attached to it (hence, for example, a place of gathering, a place of worship, a commemorative place, a restful place, *Raumgefühl*). When confronted with a particular situation—a site, program, materials, and the like—architecture's imagination enfolds all of its conditions into formal quanta, intensities, or architectemes and produces an analogue of the originary, purposeful, place-making condition of architecture.

In order for the purposeful qualities of this analogue to be put into relation, in order for the qualities to achieve expression, an autonomous system of organization is required—one that has internal consistency as well as external effect. Typology is one such system. Understood in this way, a typological analysis of architecture demands a rigorous attention to form as well as to the symbolic identification that extends outward from structure into externality and alterity in a proliferating chain of metonymic associations. This is where typology begins to trace the contours of architecture's desire. For typology's effort to grasp analytically the preanalytic and indeterminate conditions of architecture's possibility (which is to say, its Other), or, put differently, to give form to that which brings architecture into being, is analogous to the desire to assimilate the desire of the Other to oneself: "Che vuoi?" (What do you want of me?), architecture asks of its Other, folding inward to question its own identity, incorporating its own distance from itself.[6] Desire is the effort to maintain architecture as a subject together with that other world which is its surround and its origin and from which it remains forever apart.

Typology designates the paradoxical point at which architecture, whose inauguration is instrumentally directed, appears as a spontaneous, almost natural force (a residue of that originary union of form and purpose), which is not limited to any particular historical context since its exemplarity is found across places and times. The assertion of the centrality of type is, then, an assertion of the reality of architectural appearance itself (and not merely some functional cause behind it)—of the *image* of architecture (the work of type is image-ination) as its symbolic identification as architecture. Rafael Moneo forcefully generalized the importance of typology and its mediatory potential in a structured field: "To understand the question of type is to understand the nature of the architectural object today. It is a question that cannot be avoided. The architectural object can no longer be considered as a single, isolated event because it is bounded by the world that surrounds it as well as by its history. It extends life to other objects by virtue of its specific architectural condition, thereby establishing a chain of related events in which it is possible to find common formal structures."[7]

Moneo and other commentators of the period rightly place the work of Aldo Rossi at the center of this structuralization of architecture. Structuralist influences, especially of Lévi-Strauss, saturate Rossi's 1966 *The Architecture of the City*; the elemental purity and formal logic of his work—its power as appearance, image, even illusion—are its most immediately apparent qualities; Rossi himself wrote that "the points specified by Ferdinand de Saussure for the development of linguistics can be translated into a program for the development of urban science."[8] What has not been sufficiently understood is how Rossi's writings, drawings, and projects depart from and transform basic structuralist insights, refracting them through his intellectual formation in Marx and Freud, reorganizing them through his readings of Lukács and Adorno, and folding that mixture through his idiosyncratic poetics, rendering his work considerably more complex than standard structuralist-semiotic accounts can afford.

For one thing, those accounts assumed a conceptual distinction between the affirmative construction of meaning on the one hand and a grimly instrumentalist functionalism on the other, a functionalism that, if not altogether meaningless, was uncommunicative and downright unsociable. Rossi's more dialectical understanding of architecture's system, however, allowed the recognition that new architectural events, experiences, and meanings are constituted not only in the reaffirmation of preexisting cultural codes but also by the specific ways that codes can be negated—spontaneously, by the ongoing effects of reification; programmatically, by changing performative and perceptual conventions and possibilities; or by design, through the ideological practice of the architect. His recognition of the multiple modes of negativity together with his inquiry into architecture's Imaginary and Symbolic orders makes Rossi a foundational figure for a theorization of the late avant-garde.[9]

Equally important is Rossi's specific conceptualization of architecture's structure. According to the standard account, architectural structure pertains essentially to the organization of architectural signifiers among themselves. An architectural type, then, as I have said, is a kind of mediator imposed between a substratum of codes, categories, customs, and conventions and the actual instance of design practice, a mediator through whose operation an architectural form comes into being as a structured material entity. While this account in all its different forms tends to presuppose some kind of social and historical reality beyond the typological operator, which serves as the type's most distant referent (not to say as a base for its superstructure), Rossi makes the more particular claim that the social and the historical are always already within the structure itself, that structure is both form and matter, that human history produces structure, and structure yields the social. In *The Architecture of the City*, he stages this as a kind of diachronic and synchronic unification:

> In this book we have made use of the historical method from two different points of view. In the first, the city was

2.1
Aldo Rossi and Gianni Braghieri, Cemetery of
San Cataldo, Modena, 1971, plan. The Museum
of Modern Art, New York. **"The analogy with death
is possible only when dealing with the finished
object, with the end of all things."**

seen as a material artifact, a man-made object built over time and retaining the traces of time. . . . Cities become historical texts. . . . The second point of view sees history as the study of the actual formation and structure of urban artifacts. It is complementary to the first and directly concerns not only the real structure of the city but also the idea that the city is a synthesis of a series of values. Thus it concerns the collective imagination. . . . The idea of history as the structure of urban artifacts is affirmed by the continuities that exist in the deepest layers of urban structure, where certain fundamental characteristics that are common to the entire urban dynamic can be seen.[10]

The architecture of the city is the crucible of the social Imaginary, a highly differentiated condition that operates on different planes or levels of reality—among them is the structured plane of its own system of signification (what others call its deep structure, *langue*, or generative grammar), which gives architecture its autonomy; a plane of historical, material manifestations in physical form (something like an archive of all past architectural events); and a plane activated with a kind of organizing force or potential, an architecture-galvanic surface ("We can utilize the reference points of the existing city, placing them on a vast, illuminated surface: and thereby let architecture participate, little by little, in the creation of new events")[11] that keeps the whole thing in motion. But there are others too. At different places in *The Architecture of the City* Rossi isolates these various planes—in sections entitled "Monuments and the Theory of Permanences," "The Dynamic of Urban Elements," "Processes of Transformation," "Urban Ecology and Psychology," "The Collective Memory," "The City as Field of Application of Various Forces"; there are more. Typology here becomes not just a third term so much as a mobile mechanism of production and analysis that can move through all of these levels. And the ideal sum of all the planes, or laminates—that unthinkable conflation—is what Rossi calls the "City," which I capitalize here to signal its singular, almost mythical, status. For the City is architecture's big Other—the order of the architectural-social Symbolic itself operating behind the typological Imaginary.[12]

A city, of course, is a sociomaterial object that we can experience and study directly, the most concrete of realities that architecture deals with. But for Rossi the City is an invisible and absent abstraction, an autonomous and presuppositional structure, a network of pure virtuality that nevertheless produces not only form but also moods, atmospheres, and affections. In his *Scientific Autobiography*, Rossi refers to the City as the very possibility of joining images, "a circle" of relationships "that is never closed," "the unlimited *contamination* of things, of correspondences"; the City is a desiring production of correspondences and connections whose quarry is anamorphosis and shadow.[13] The City is the object of architecture's desire prior to any predication, which nevertheless enables and constrains every possible architectural creation and can be known through its architectural effects. While the City cannot be deduced from any single example of architecture, and every possible analogue of the City is necessarily partial and often contradictory, there is nevertheless no architecture that is not determined and legitimated by the City, which is the very structure of architecture's tradition. For Rossi the City is something very like an architectural unconscious—the Other as both embodiment of the social substance and the site of the unconscious. In this regard it is interesting to recall Lacan's famous quip, "The best image to sum up the unconscious is Baltimore in the early morning."[14] But with this it is important to add that Rossi, like Lacan, insists that this unconscious is precisely not subjective, not something with any individual psychic makeup. Rather, the architectural unconscious is outside and collective, in the domain and material of signification itself.

We can learn more about the concept of the City by isolating two related but different kinds of time operating in Rossi's peculiar theory of typology, two different temporal logics. First is the analysis of variance in what might be called the phenomenon of typological repetition and persistence. Herein lies the importance of Rossi's notion of "permanences," which tries to account for the persistence of certain spatial patterns in the urban fabric as material "signs of the past" as well as the persistence of a city's basic plan over vast periods of time and changes in use, even when monuments or sectors of a city are destroyed just to be rebuilt exactly as they were. The examples in *The Architecture of the City* are many, but Rossi dwells particularly on the large and complex Palazzo della Ragione in Padua and how it has successfully accommodated and encouraged different functions since the fifteenth century. Another case is the Roman amphitheater at Nîmes, which was transformed first into a fortress and then a small city of two thousand, with four gates and two churches inside its original walls. Both are examples of "propelling permanences," catalytic elements of the city whose powerful forms remain stable but whose functional variability contribute to the evolving process of urbanization and the production of new architectural experiences. There may also be "pathological permanences"—the Alhambra in Granada is Rossi's example—that function only as isolated, unalterable obstructions in the city, restricting rather than propelling programmatic differentiation.[15]

The correlate of typological persistence is another kind of chronicity that may be called the anteriority of typology, a logic of prelusion and process, of coming before. With this terminology I mean to capture the sense of mimetic folding and refolding of preexisting forms in Rossi's often-cited but exceedingly elliptical illustration of the "analogous city," which describes the originary site of architecture's symbolization:

> To illustrate this concept I gave the example of Canaletto's fantasy view of Venice, a capriccio in which Palladio's projects for the Ponte di Rialto, the Basilica of Vicenza, and the Palazzo Chiericati are set next to each other and described as if the painter were rendering an urban scene he had actually observed. These three Palladian monuments, none of which are actually in Venice (one is a project; the other two are in Vicenza), nevertheless constitute an analogous Venice formed of specific elements associated with the history of both architecture and the city. The geographical transposition of the monuments within the painting constitutes a city that we recognize, even though it is a place of purely architectural references. This example enabled me to demonstrate how a logical-formal operation could be translated into a design method and then into a hypothesis for a theory of architectural design in which the elements were preestablished and formally defined, but where the significance that sprung forth at the end of the operation was the authentic, unforeseen, and original meaning of the work.[16]

There is an epistemological claim made in this formulation insofar as the analogue is at once a means of analysis, a method of design, and a necessary prior condition for practice. Indeed, as a means of knowing, Rossi's concept of analogy has a remarkable closeness to Lévi-Strauss's *pensée sauvage*. For Lévi-Strauss's complex and multimodal mind also responds to its situation on many levels simultaneously and "builds mental structures which facilitate an understanding of the world in as much as they resemble it. In this sense savage thought can be defined as

2.2
Aldo Rossi, *La scuola di Fagnano Olona.*
Altre relazioni, 1979, sketch.
Courtesy Fondazione Aldo Rossi.

analogical thought."[17] Analogical thought sorts the world into a series of structured oppositions and then proposes that each set of oppositions is analogically related to other sets insofar as their differences resemble one another. In Rossi's project for the Modena cemetery (1971), for example, the difference between the individual tomb and the cemetery as a whole is the same as the difference between a house and a city, whereas the conic communal grave and the cubic die that is the sanctuary for the war dead are similarly analogous to the monuments and permanences of a city: homologies between systems of difference, isomorphic diagrams.[18] Dimensions are of no importance in analogical thought since the order of the City is cognitively embedded in all architectural types of any scale. Rossi speaks of Diocletian's Palace at Split, Croatia, as an example: "Split discovered in its own typological form an entire city, and thus the building came to refer analogically to the form of a city. This example is evidence that a single building can be designed by analogy to the city."[19] Exactly the same analogy is present in Rossi's own designs, such as the elementary school at Fagnano Olona (1972–1976)—itself a small city with hallway-streets, piazza, public rotunda, and monumental steps—and even his drawings of "domestic landscapes," which organize cigarette packs, tea pots, and furniture like urban fragments.[20]

In this epistemological claim, the anteriority of typology is entirely consistent with the structuralist attempt to work out a theory of models constructed on the analogy with language, and with the presupposition that all thought must be conducted through and within the limits of an objective field in which every element occupies a preordained place. In a sense, the anteriority of types is a fundamentally Kantian conception (as is much of structuralism's underpinning). For if architecture is structured like conceptual-objective thought itself and is an activity whose content is determinately social and socially useful, it is precisely because architectural types mimic conceptual processes and social content at the level of form. Or, to put it in an even more Kantian way, the logic of types is autonomous in the sense that it provides the form for conceptual thought and social experience rather than being determined by them. Types "facilitate an understanding of the world in as much as they resemble it" (Lévi-Strauss). It is through this kind of thinking that we can understand, for example, Rossi's fascination with Adolf Loos's aphorism, "If we find a mound six feet long and three feet wide in the forest, formed into a pyramid, shaped by a shovel, we become serious and something in us says, 'someone lies buried here.' That is architecture."[21] The particular architectural image of the mound—the analogue—produces the affect of reverence. Rossi concludes, "The mound six feet long and three feet wide is an extremely intense and pure architecture precisely because it is identifiable in the artifact. It is only in the history of architecture that a separation between the original element and its various forms occurred. From this separation, which the ancient world seemingly resolved forever, derives the universally acknowledged character of permanence of those first forms."[22]

But if there is an elective affinity between the language of type and the social world, there is also an opacity, an unbridgeable gap revealed in type's analogical work. Think of the different sameness of the cube in Rossi's Cuneo, Modena, and Teatro del Mondo projects, or the repetitive walls of Modena's ossuaries, the same type as the wall of apartments in the Gallaratese. Think of the way these figures open to a singularity and a difference that cannot be subsumed within the rule of representation. Rossi recounts an exchange between Freud and Carl Jung, in which the later explains that "'logical' thought is what is expressed in words directed to the outside world in the form of discourse. 'Analogical' thought is sensed yet unreal, imagined yet silent; it is not a discourse but rather a mediation on theses of the past, an interior monologue.

Logical thought is 'thinking in words.' Analogical thought is archaic, unexpressed, and practically inexpressible in words."[23] A type, logical and analogical at the same time, perpetually excludes what it seeks to possess, which is its own identity as conferred by the City. *That is its desire.* This alone explains why Rossi's work, in all its dismaying aesthetic impoverishment, compels commentators to declare that it produces memories. Rossi himself insists as much in his elaboration on the above quotation: "I believe I have found in this definition [of analogy] a different sense of history conceived not simply as fact but rather as a series of things, of affective objects to be used by the memory or in design."[24] The radical lack at the heart of desire is scanned as "memory" by the mind habituated to language.

Rossi's concept of analogy also makes an ontological claim: architecture can come only from architecture. A type is cataphoric and anaphoric, pointing backward and forward at the same time. But typology's schematization cannot gather up all that is the City; the system of types may claim to be the epistemological infrastructure but not the ontological ground of architecture. What is anterior to all typology, then, is simply the dialectical fact that architecture constitutes itself in relation to what is not architecture. For its autonomy, in other words, architecture requires something heteronomous. According to Rossi, that something is the social itself. Of course, all of architecture emerges from a historical and social context, but Rossi's formulation is more particular. Consider *The Architecture of the City*'s concluding paragraph, in which the City's order is given a biographical-biological characterization as an apparatus that regulates identifications and relations with other subjects and objects and then remains as a record: "Perhaps the laws of the city are exactly like those that regulate the life and destiny of individual men. Every biography has its own interest, even though it is circumscribed by birth and death. Certainly the architecture of the city, the human thing par excellence, is the physical sign of this biography, beyond the meanings and feelings with which we recognize it."[25] Rossi makes a similar point elsewhere: "Architecture is the most important of the arts and sciences, because its cycle is natural like the cycle of man, but it is what *remains* of man."[26]

The City contains social relations within its structure, but unconsciously, so to speak (the unconscious is the "discourse of the Other"), while at the same time positing an ideal regulatory set of relationships that exceeds any origin. And typological practice takes as its privileged object just the social, economic, and psychological forms that organize urban life at all of its levels and against which individual architectural proposals take place and become comprehensible. The type is thus a doubled thing. The City is a palimpsest of the marks left by the events of human history, a "biographical" diagram. The City's facts, layers of the palimpsest, are cognitive forms revealed in artifacts, constituting what Rossi calls the "individualità del fatto urbano"— the singularity of the urban event—by which he signals not just a physical thing and its formal logic but also any city's existential life. Thus typology is, first, a record, a trace, a presentation of those marks of events that allows them to be most fully experienced and comprehended, rendering thinkable situations otherwise given only in affective terms. And the City can be thought of as the medium or matrix in which particular types are suspended and vehiculated. Second, it is the instrument—the "apparatus," Rossi calls it—that analyzes and operates on this medium and material of any city's history.

> *Such an argument presupposes that the architectural artifact is conceived as a structure and that this structure is revealed and can be recognized in the artifact itself. As a constant, this principle, which we can call the typical element, or simply the type, is to be found in all architec-*

tural artifacts. It is also then a cultural element and as such can be investigated in different architectural artifacts; typology becomes in this way the analytical moment of architecture, and it becomes readily identifiable at the level of urban artifacts.[27]

If we now take the epistemological and ontological claims together, we can further understand typology as nothing less than a study of superstructures, understood as involving mental processes as well as cultural products. And if we ask again about the operations by which such ideational and cultural materials might be linked up with sociomaterial reality, then an architectural type reveals itself as an intermediary object between thought and reality, "a structure that is revealed and made knowledgeable through the fact itself."[28] As immanent analysis of City, the logic of types is dedicated to a full engagement with reality's tones, textures, and rhythms, as much as its formal elements and syntaxes. As representational apparatus, an architectural type transmits the contours and movements of an otherwise remote and inexpressible historical reality and presents them for analysis. Formal rigor is maintained and extended into the social and back again, or better, architectural form exists as cognitive object and process in a social constellation. But it is important to insist here that, different from substantive theories of meaning or structure, Rossi's type requires a certain kind of circular and negative thinking: a type does not symbolize; nor does it convey a positive "meaning." Rather, a type *appears as symbolized*, which is to say that it appears as an analogy and a presentation of a determining Symbolic order that is itself unrepresentable and forever out of reach.

"Only a form closed and concluded [*chiusa e conchiusa*], *l'opera definita*, is the concrete measure of the dimension that surrounds it,"[29] Rossi claims. He is most likely responding in the passage to

Umberto Eco's *Opera aperta* (1962) and its metaphorical use in urban design, but he might as well have been thinking of Adorno, who elaborates a similar point in his famous 1957 essay "On Lyric Poetry and Society," in which he admonishes that interpretation "may not focus directly on the so-called social perspective or the social interests of the works or their authors. Instead, it must discover how the entirety of a society, conceived as an internally contradictory unity, is manifested in the work of art. . . . Nothing that is not in works of art or aesthetic theory themselves, not part of their own form, can legitimate a determination [*Entscheidung*] of what their substance, that which has entered into their poetry, represents in social terms."[30] For Rossi, it seems that what was an external line of impingement between superstructural and ideational phenomena such as architecture and the material substance of the base becomes in the City an internal distinction, perhaps like Adorno's microanalysis; for the City carries within itself both superstructure and infrastructure, both culture and history, both process and raw material. In his foundational study of Rossi, Moneo put this succinctly in terms of the autonomy of architecture in the city: "Through the idea of autonomy, necessary to the understanding of the form of the city, architecture becomes a category of reality."[31]

Our discussion of the anteriority of type as a temporal logic now turns back on and complicates the corollary phenomenon of typological persistence. For the enabling, organizing, architecturally identifying force of the City is anterior to and determinate of all architecture—the necessary condition and prelude to all practice—and the objects and events produced out of the City's conditions of possibility trace the latent or repressed reality of this Symbolic order, reoriginating its forms in new situations wrested free from the City's necessity. But the objects and events, the types, thus produced then return their forms (cognitive structures that mimic the social) to the City's matrix and persist in surroundings utterly alien to them—analogues of a single, unfinished architectural narrative, a great collective story whose end, for Rossi, is as impossible to achieve as its process is necessary to perform: hence his relentless repetition and substitution of types. "Now it seems to me that everything has already been seen; when I design I repeat, and in the observation of things there is also the observation of memory. I design my projects with a discrete sense of affection for each one but I reduce them to things that surround me; country houses, smoke stacks, monuments and objects, as if everything arose from and was founded in time; in this beginnings and endings are confounded."[32]

Critics of Rossi have often detected in his ceaseless repetitions of images a nostalgia for a lost ideal order or perhaps even a mourning for that loss.[33] What is more, the defining characteristics of his projects—extreme ambiguities of scale; juxtapositions of incommensurable objects seemingly forced by the architect into some silent, secret dialogue; the sense of separateness and fixity radiated by the elemental objects in metaphysical cityscapes, lit by a light that seems to consume all substance—all these should be read as results of the radical unavailability of the City's Symbolic order to the individual types that desire to posses it. The types persist, torn from themselves, because of this lack; desire itself persists because of this lack.

The phenomenon of persistence must therefore be read as an ambiguous or paradoxical logic—not just of enduring after a beginning (a physical form being newly occupied and experienced beyond its original usefulness and contextual integrity) but also of persisting after an end, the survival of form beyond what should have been its point of exhaustion. Think of the library rotunda of the elementary school at Fagnano Olona and especially of the black-and-white photographs that are always its privileged presentation. To become a library, the rotunda must negate its origins as baptistery or theater. But Rossi rejects these

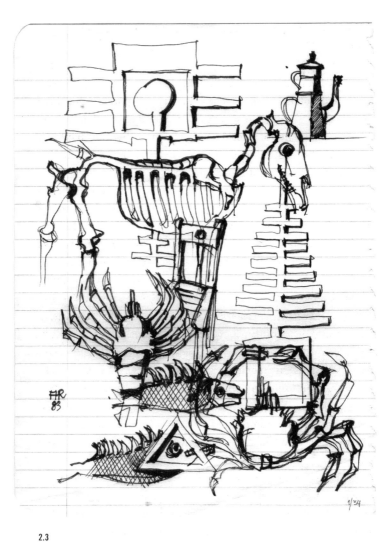

2.3
Aldo Rossi, untitled, 1983, sketch.
Courtesy Fondazione Aldo Rossi.
The plans in the sketch are of the
school at Fagnano Olona and the
cemetery at Modena.

handed-down meanings with a formal reduction and negation so radical that it appears not simply to transform the rotunda type from one use to another but to elevate meaninglessness itself in place of meaning, and absence and lack in place of presence. Moneo comments on the resultant formal-temporal confusion of the school: "Do not the schoolchildren of Fagnano Olona look like the inhabitants of a world not their own? The children inhabit a time that already alludes more to what will become their own past than to the present arrested by the photograph."[34]

In Rossi's highly reflexive relation to the crisis of meaning announced by Baird, Jencks, and others, meaning inheres in the negation of meaning and the negation of meaning takes shape as a fragmentation and evacuation of form, leaving persistent images that Rossi's critics have found haunted, silent, nonidentical, and disturbing. Many have tried to assuage this atmospheric untimeliness with references to the oneiric realism of De Chirico and the *neue Sachlichkeit*. Others have pointed out that, rather than merely picking out formal similarities that existed antecedently, Rossi's constructions in fact create anew and sometimes even confuse the very typological analogies on which they claim to depend. Alan Colquhoun once remarked that Fagnano Olona was not based on anything in architecture's formal history but had rather constituted "a pure type that has not yet entered the history of which it is a model."[35] And Anthony Vidler invites us, somewhat ominously, to consider another example, Rossi's Trieste City Hall project, in light of associated implications characteristic of its type, which is that of a late-eighteenth-century prison: "The dialectic is clear as a fable: the society that understands the reference to prison will still have need of the reminder, while at the very point the image finally loses all meaning, the society will either have become entirely prison, or, perhaps, its opposite."[36] In every case, even in these brief comments, there hovers over the work a dreadful sense of an architecture out of time—remaining, lingering, living on after its legitimacy and rightfulness have passed. Wilhelm Worringer long ago associated abstraction with "an immense spiritual dread of space."[37] Rossi's work is figural on the other side of abstraction and induces a dread that seems to extend not only to space but also to time.

No one has grasped the radical anachronicity of Rossi's work better than Peter Eisenman. In an essay entitled "The House of the Dead as the City of Survival," Eisenman weaves a historicist-psychoanalytic interpretation of a suite of drawings by Rossi that Eisenman refers to as *Città Analoga*. He first gives a concise summation of the analogue's relation to history—"In one sense, the analogue uses history, that is, what is existing, to order what will be new. At the same time it is ahistorical in that it cuts off the formative stages of the process. In its denial of historical generation it replicates the present condition of history (without its history)"—and then anchors the historicity of the ahistorical, if you will, precisely in the historical moment of the 1970s.

> *Rossi's "rationalism" conjoins the post-1945 condition of man. And to characterize his images as "neo-classical" or "rationalist" in the traditional sense is to ignore this conjunction. For their special rationality, which consists in the combination of logic—the conscious—with the analogic—the shadow—is not necessarily to be found in their conscious imagery. Rossi's conscious images exist only as a key to their shadow imagery. It is their intrinsic, often unconscious content which confronts the more problematic and perhaps fundamental reality of the extrinsic cultural condition today.*[38]

In articulating the constitutive absence (the shadow, the unconscious) of the City, Eisenman is characteristically mining the Hegelian insight that each artwork is symbol and sole inhabitant

of a world that is nonetheless implied by the very achieved singularity of the artwork's existence. Hence the alienation of work
like Rossi's. For the artwork is the dislocated, displaced, and
singular example of a world that cannot otherwise bring itself
into existence more completely and must remain largely absent
and incomplete. Rossi maintains the world-constructing desire
of the modern avant-garde, but he is condemned by *this* world—
by posthistory—to repeat the same analogically rather than to
follow modernism's frequently twinned impulse of utopian future
countergesture. The new cannot appear as such in Rossi's work;
it can appear only as an unrepresentable negative totality, the
comprehension of which must take the form of Adorno's micro-
logical analysis of architectural fragments and ruins.[39]

Eisenman indeed comes very close also to Adorno's post-
Holocaust art thesis—that after Auschwitz there can be no before
Auschwitz. Our encounter with art is on the ground of a trauma
and an impasse so extreme that it leaves no space for meaningful
resolution. The conviction of Eisenman's writing, which defies
paraphrase, warrants quoting at length:

> *The events of 1945, the full comprehension of the meaning
> of the Holocaust and atomic destruction, have changed
> the bases on which life can be lived. For man faced with a
> choice between imminent or eventual mass death, hero-
> ism, whether individual or collective, is untenable: only
> survival remains possible. The problem is now of choosing
> between an anachronistic continuance of hope and an
> acceptance of the bare conditions of survival. And when
> the hero can be only a survivor, there is no choice. The
> condition of man which formerly contained this alter-
> native has ended, and the continuous "narrative" of the
> progress of Western civilization has been broken.*[40]

According to Eisenman, the end is already behind us and architecture is always already surviving its own death, a testimony to its own anachronicity. As a survivor, architecture is condemned to afterlife and aftermath, implying both the post-finitum as well as the fatal repetition compulsion (which we consider shortly). Perhaps Eisenman's concluding paragraph is not too hyperbolic. Rossi's "is an architecture which confronts the reality of the present. His drawings offer 'nothing new' precisely because anything new which can be offered is, in the present condition, nothing. They simply ask, however anxiously, for the existence of a choice between life as survival, and death."[41] Had Eisenman known Adorno's famous formulation of the logic of living on after the end, he surely would have appropriated it for architecture: "Philosophy, which once seemed obsolete, lives on because the moment to realize it was missed."[42]

Eisenman's reading of Rossi's analogous architecture brings us to the brink where the architectural Imaginary is disrupted by an intrusion of the Real. For when architecture's symbolic efficiency is in doubt, when the stability of its Other is undermined, the Imaginary itself starts to collapse. And yet at this brink we are also able to ask the question, What then is architecture's Real? and to answer with one powerful word: History. For the City, architecture's symbolic mandate, its necessity, is not some content but rather the inexorable form of human events, the outcome of a vast human process. The City is the architectural form taken by historical necessity. And while form grants architecture a certain freedom, History enforces its reinscription in the fated repetition of the same. Whence come the numerous negations that every critic of Rossi has stumbled on: ruins, abandonments, destructions, dissolutions, an entire canon of negativity, the importance of which will be, above all, not a declaration of architecture's end but of the kernel of History installed at its core. So it is not the case that the anteriority of type is a beginning that has the endurance of types as its end but rather that both have been shifted from states to processes that operate together as modes of delay. Architecture has no end because it is a permanent movement through time—a persistent differential. Architecture uses its difference and its autonomy to manage the heteronomous historical and social forces that inhere in architecture as a social product but in a way that allows the repressed social forms of the material to be known and experienced. If such a process leads to necessary failure, then that is in no way the result of technical inadequacy. Rather, it comes from the structural impossibility of succeeding in the task thus faced—a truth to the historical demands of the material—a task that must nevertheless be undertaken.

REPETITION

Peter Eisenman begins his introduction to the 1982 English translation of Aldo Rossi's *The Architecture of the City* with an excerpt from Jacques Derrida's *Writing and Difference:* **"The relief and design of structures appears more clearly when content, which is the living energy of meaning, is neutralized, somewhat like the architecture of an uninhabited or deserted city, reduced to its skeleton by some catastrophe of nature or art.** A city no longer inhabited, not simply left behind, but haunted by meaning and culture, this state of being haunted, which keeps the city from returning to nature."[1] The passage facilitates a shift of Rossi's theory of the city toward poststructuralism and psychoanalysis (do we not hear echoes in the quotation of *Civilization and Its Discontents*?) and gives Eisenman a way to assimilate Rossi's aphoristic mention of skeletons and fractures to his own rhetoric of the unhappy consciousness that is powerfully terminal, at times even apocalyptic.[2] For Eisenman the skeleton is an object identical to its structure, a system consistent with itself rather than corresponding to some remote referent. It nevertheless has a determinate history; indeed, it is "at once a structure and a ruin, a record of events and a record of time," an object-become-simulacrum-of-process. It is self-reflexive, "for it is also an object that can be used to study its own structure," a structure of individual elements within a generalized framework.[3] But it is divided within itself insofar as it can determine itself (each of its elements) only through the differential relations enabled by that structure, which are the structure's effects. Eisenman is particularly taken with this osteo-logical machinery of relational elements and structuring grid—uninhabited, haunted by its own history, constituted in difference rather than identity. It is because in his brooding over Rossi's idea of City, he has uncovered something of his own.

More than any contemporary architect, Eisenman has sought a space for architecture outside the traditional parameters of the sensual and the built, the phenomenological and the practical. In projects and writings between 1966 and 1985, he sought nothing less than architecture's *Ursprung*—the primordial flow of signifi-cation he variously referred to as architecture's "deep structure," "autonomy," and "interiority"—which he found both irreducible and aporetic. Near the end of that search Eisenman posed the question this way:

> *What can be the model for architecture when the essence of what was effective in the classical model—the presumed rational value of structures, representations, methodolo-gies of origins and ends, and deductive processes—has been shown to be a simulation? It is not possible to answer such a question with an alternative model. But a series of characteristics can be proposed that typify this aporia, this loss in our capacity to conceptualize a new model for architecture. These characteristics . . . arise from that which can not be; they form a structure of absences.*[4]

Eisenman is thinking here of a series of projects he called the "cities of artificial excavation," experiments undertaken from 1978 to 1988 that enact a kind of Derridean archi-writing, in which the very possibility of producing architectural mean-ing through the tracing, grafting, and scaling of geometric deep structures of specific sites—Venice, Berlin, Paris, Long Beach—

also decenters and unravels the certainty of that meaning, re-quiring the supplementation of authors and authorities from Le Corbusier to Shakespeare to the sites' own histories; supplementation, indeed, backward and forward to infinity, although the past is not recoverable and the coming of the future has been pitilessly stalled.[5] "Architecture in the present is seen as a process of inventing an artificial past and a futureless present. It remembers a no-longer future."[6] The cities of artificial excavation thus lead inexorably beyond the end of the line of architecture, to "the end of the end."

I shall be concerned here with that end and its logic, and with the architectural drawing as its iteration. I discuss what may properly be called conceptual architecture—one that seeks through an aesthetic withdrawal to replace the built object with a diagram of its formative procedures, investigating, exposing, and repeating the most basic disciplinary conventions and techniques of architectural practice while at the same time liquidating the last vestiges of sensual architectural experience. I shall be concerned, in particular, with the 1978 project for the Cannaregio district of Venice, the first of the cities of artificial excavation. My intention is to query not only the conceptual workings of this architecture but also its historicity—how it is a conscious reflection on a particular cultural moment—and to develop an etiology of self-reflexive formalism that can identify the historical illness of which, I will claim, Eisenman's architecture (along with others of the late avant-garde) is an elaborate symptom. The illness, not to make a mystery of it, is *reification*: a kind of epistemic anomie that results from the systematic fragmentation, quantification, and depletion of every realm of subjective experience, but understood here also as an effect in the architectural material itself. In Eisenman's cities of artificial excavation, the contours of that historical condition remain legible after all other meanings have been hollowed out.

Eisenman affirmed early on that if ever there were to be a cure, it would be a resolutely formal one. Before 1978 his work was concerned almost exclusively with isolating and elaborating the architectural elements and operations that would ensure the autonomy and self-reflexivity of the architectural object, which would verify and purify itself in resistance to all encircling determinants of architectural form. One such determinant is physical construction. Eisenman's notion of "cardboard" architecture unloads the physical object of all traditional senses of building with stable materials. Another is the building's actual use. Eisenman's postfunctionalism shifts our engagement with form from utilization to a consideration of architectural elements as the material support of signals or notations for a conceptual state of the object. A final determinant is all the contextual, narrative, or associational potentials of built form. Eisenman's emphasis on the syntactic over the semantic dimension of form proposes on behalf of the architect and the viewer a "competence," or knowledge of the discipline—understood as an internalized system of architectural principles and underlying rules of combination—and stresses the deep, conceptual structures from which various architectures can be generated over the sensual, surface characteristics of any built instance.[7] Eisenman's early work thus incorporates two standard structuralist principles: the bracketing off of the physical and historical context and, with that, the bracketing off of the subject in favor of a notion of an intersubjective structure of architectural signification that, like language, predates any individual and is much less his or her product than he or she is the effect of it.

We have been taught to think of this as "mere" formalism. But in House I through House VI (1969–1972), Eisenman follows the modernist strategies of distancing, defamiliarization, and deployment of an alienation effect (from Bertolt Brecht's *Verfremdungseffekt*) to reorient our apprehension of architectural form away from standard perceptual conventions. In a traditional representational architecture whose form has its referent in, say, the human body, traditional or indigenous constructions, or some preformed classical system of meaning, our attention as viewers is drawn not to the *act* of representing—not to how the particular object has been conceived and constructed, from what kind of position and with what end in view—but simply to what is already there, the referent that stands before and external to the architectural sign. Any traditional or conventional form is likely to have more authority, to engage our assent more readily, than a form that tries to expose the complex matrix of disciplinary procedures and institutional apparatuses through which the object is actually constructed. Part of the power of such a representational architecture lies in its suppression of its procedures of production, of how it got to be what it is. Strategies of defamiliarization and estrangement, by contrast, attempt to make the processes of the object's production and the mechanisms of its representation part of its content. The object does not attempt to pass itself off as unquestionable, but rather to lay bare the devices of its own formation so that the viewer will be encouraged to reflect critically on the particular, partial ways in which it is constituted, the particular ways it takes its place.

Eisenman situates his work in a line descending from modernist defamiliarization practices, producing in the early houses a state of estrangement that corresponds to the absolute divorce of form from all reference to materiality, use, and association. In an explanation of House III, significantly entitled "To Adolf Loos & Bertolt Brecht," Eisenman confirms his Loosian sense of *Raumgefühl* and Brechtian understanding of the *Verfremdungseffekt*:

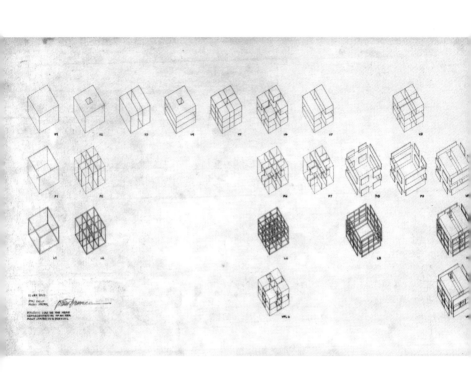

3.1
Peter Eisenman, House IV transformation
study, multiple axonometrics, 1975.
The Museum of Modern Art, New York.

> While the architectural system may be complete, the
> environment "house" is almost a void. And quite unin-
> tentionally—like the audience of the film—the owner has
> been alienated from his environment. In this sense, when
> the owner first enters "his house" he is an intruder; he
> must begin to regain possession—to occupy a foreign con-
> tainer. In the process of taking possession the owner be-
> gins to destroy, albeit in a positive sense, the initial unity
> and completeness of the architectural structure. . . . By
> acting in response to a given structure, the owner is now
> almost working against this pattern. By working to come
> to terms with this structure, design is not decoration but
> rather becomes a process of inquiry into one's own latent
> capacity to understand any man-made space.[8]

This passage emphasizes the identification of an independent
conceptual notational system distanced both from any external
referent and from any determinable individual viewer. The object
and its elements—the cube in its particular emblematic status, the
fundamental units of plane, volume, and frame and their mutual
interactions—are foregrounded as an architectural writing, one
that is *scriptible* in Barthes's sense (he also follows Brecht here) of
not only revealing and insisting on its own constructedness but
also inviting, requiring even, a reciprocal productive activity of
the reader or viewer.[9] Now, in recognizing that the architectural
object adequately names that which propels the activity of viewing, reading, and rescripting—propels, that is, any possible
viewer's recognition and repetition of disciplinarily structured
modes of interpretation—we have broached a notion of performativity, understood in the sense that the object-as-performative-
production constitutes that which in the object-as-representation
always escapes us. Thus, "working to come to terms with this
structure"—the reading and rewriting or rearchitecting of the

performative production—means trying to make sense not only of the formal object but also of the perceptual conventions and disciplinary institutions that it activates and, in activating, *repeats*. Conformity to these conventions and institutions is precipitated, it must be underscored, by the architectural object itself in its structured reiterability. Thus is the object moved to a reflexivity of a second order.

In the Cannaregio project, we witness a similar second-order shift that begins the cities of artificial excavation and establishes the theme that henceforth characterizes Eisenman's work: the movement from structure to site to text, or, better, from the structuralization of the object to the textualization of site.[10] This movement is a consequence of the alienation effects mentioned above and the performativity or scriptability of the object, taking these to their conclusion in a self-critique of the fundamental techniques and procedures of the discipline of architecture that the early works had attempted to isolate and codify, but now with a sense that History itself has radically changed the conditions of possibility for any effectiveness of critique. After the end of the end, architecture's iterability loops in on itself, redoubling to produce a temporality in which architectural objects are dislocated and internally split—an intrinsic condition of the late avant-garde, which Eisenman called architecture's presentness: "More than any other term, [*presentness*] combines both the idea of time in presence, of the experience of space in the present, while at the same time its suffix -*ness* causes a distance between the object as presence, which is a given in architecture, and the quality of that presence as time, which may be something other than mere presence."[11] What is left for an architecture that would trace that "structure of absences," that would "remember a no-longer future," is then nothing but a totality of infinite deferral. All of which will leave us in an uncompromising place indeed, one in which any positive or substantive construal of the archi-

3.2
Peter Eisenman, project for Cannaregio, 1978, plan.
Courtesy of the architect. **"Upon close examination
these objects reveal that they contain nothing—they
are solid, lifeless blocks which seem to have been
formerly attached to the context. . . . They leave
a trace, mark the absence of their former presence;
their presence is nothing but an absence."**

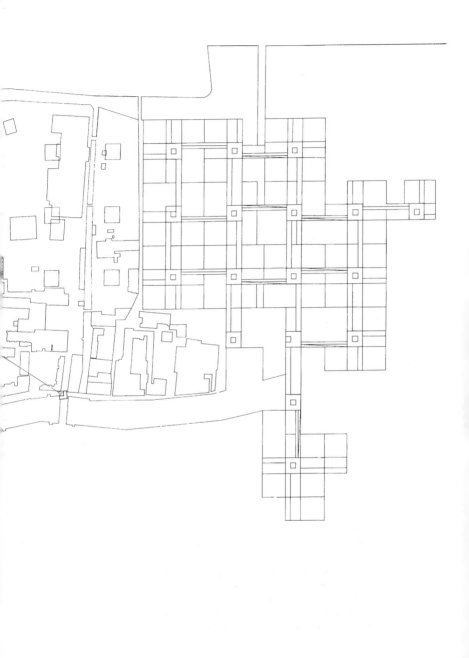

tect's own negative method is refused (any effort to represent a "better" past or future, for example), but which at the same time also refuses to cancel the representational project as such. Thus Eisenman understands our most elaborate imaginative efforts to conjure alternatives or to propose the next New as little more than projections out of our own historical predicament.

Cannaregio is the first of Eisenman's projects in which the site becomes a major factor in the signifying practice. The grid of Le Corbusier's unrealized Venice hospital project (1964–1965), his last design before his death—itself an absent emblem of the utopian, salutary ambition of modern architecture and, at the same time, a rationalization of the ad hoc urban structure of Venice—is reduced to a geometrical abstraction and folded over onto the irregular fabric of the adjacent site. Here we have for the first time, then, not only an incorporation of the immediate context into the structure of the work, but also an important new operation: that of *appropriation* and the concomitant nullification of the confiscated object's semantic qualities. Le Corbusier's project is reduced to a series of voids, holes in the ground, hollowed out so utterly that only an imprint of the material remains, calibrated and reiterated to become a procedure of inscription and repetition rather than an identifiable figure (even a figure as abstract and reduced as one of Rossi's types).

But the exact status of Le Corbusier's hospital confounds the reader, for in his redrawing of the hospital in the Cannaregio presentation, Eisenman renders Le Corbusier's project with precisely the same sort of line as his own presumably "real" proposal for the site, neither ghosted nor put into quotations pictorially: there is no graphic distinction between objects proposed but not yet realized and those proposed but never to be. Does Eisenman's project for Cannaregio then mean to include the "rebuilding" of Le Corbusier's never-built monument to the modern? Or do the documents and their codes of representation declare (or condemn) Eisenman's project to be of the same never-to-be-built status, the same failed utopia? In any case, such a graphic convention makes sense only if the project is understood to be a drawing *as such* and not a drawn representation of a hypothetical building construction; it is the *drawing* of Le Corbusier's hospital in Cannaregio that is the site of Eisenman's project. In the absence of a real place to begin, Eisenman reproduces the missing original in hallucinated form, not as an object of architectural desire but as a setting for the emplacement of a Symbolic order that is also a realm of absence and lack.

For Eisenman, Le Corbusier's drawing seems to grant a provisional stability to the otherwise endless drift of the Symbolic. The dead authority returns as drawing and contract—Name-of-the-Father, the pact among initiates that controls communication, the operator that links unassuaged desire to rule.[12] The centrality of drawing as drawing for Eisenman's problematic, and indeed for that of the entire late avant-garde, is not merely the result of economic contingencies or an inability to get projects built. It is rather that drawing is the necessary vehicle of imagination, symbolization, and self-reflection in architecture, analogous to writing in language; drawing is perhaps the necessary medium of *critical* architecture. Drawing is a medium of marks that have passed from the architectural unconscious through the signifier, thus enabling and controlling signification. The drawing is indeed a privileged signifier because it alone inaugurates the process of architectural signification.

Drawing is therefore also involved in architecture's desire and hence with the City. Bernard Tschumi once remarked of Antonio Sant'Elia that

> the intensity of urban life had once been the ultimate object of desire; now it loses its fascination. The city is less important than its image . . . Sant'Elia brilliantly

3.3
Peter Eisenman, Cannaregio, 1978,
sketch site plan showing disposition
of el-cube structures with grid
derived from Le Corbusier's hospital
and diagonal axis of symmetry.
Canadian Centre for Architecture.

formalized desires. *If he is not the first to replace architecture by its drawings, he certainly replaces the reality of
the city by drawings of the city. And not of any city, but of
the city of the future, promised by new technologies and
socio-economic relations, yet inaccessible. His drawings
. . . disregard the object of desire and replace it with a
powerful substitute: drawing.*[13]

Drawing operates as metaphor, as a substitute for the desire produced by the City itself. What is more, drawing and desire are
closely related even at the level of the word, as W. J. T. Mitchell
has so suggestively argued. "'Drawing Desire' [the title of Mitchell's
essay], then, is meant not just to indicate the depiction of a scene
or figure that stands for desire but also to indicate the way that
drawing itself, the dragging or pulling of the drawing instrument,
is the *performance of desire*. Drawing draws us on. Desire just *is*,
quite literally, drawing, or *a* drawing—a pulling or attracting
force, and the trace of this force in a picture."[14]

When Eisenman decided to begin (again)—to draw from, to draw
on Le Corbusier's drawing—he could not have known Derrida's
contemporaneous account of the irreducibility of repetition
in "Limited Inc a b c" (1977).[15] Uncannily, Eisenman enacts what
Derrida simultaneously articulates: any text can come into being
only as a certain repetition, in terms of what it repeats and what
repeats it. But what is repeated (in this case a canonic modernist project) can never be self-present (and it is important for
Eisenman that Le Corbusier's project is literally absent), either
in itself or in the text that repeats it. A *coming after* (hints of
Rossi's "persistence") here emerges as the only condition under
which anything can *come to be*. Iterability displaces the logic of
self-presence by a graphics of deferral and differentiation that
Derrida famously called "spacing," or *différance*. What is more,
the superposition of Le Corbusier's grid onto the new site is a

quite vivid example of the Derridean concepts of supplement and graft. Read as supplement, Eisenman's attachment makes apparent the "originary lack" at the core of the modernist project.[16] As graft, the setting of the two Cannaregio projects side by side generates resonances, distortions, and phase shifts both formal and historical that are themselves explorations of iterability and dissemination. The Cannaregio project declares that one cannot simply bring architecture into being; one can only trace the possibility of its being repeated.

But there are logics other than Derridean that I want to explore in the effort to define the territories of deprivation and loss within this field of geometrical, indexical forms. What figures can be adduced to capture the movement from the decontextualized structuring principles of the early houses to the site-specific appropriations and repetitions in Venice? First, it can be noted that this appropriation and consequent formal and semantic depletion of Le Corbusier's project follows in its general logic of transformation what Walter Benjamin, in his study of *Trauerspiel*, identified as the figure of allegory. Allegory appears in periods of crisis, when, through metaphysical or historical causes, some unspeakable loss is imposed on what had been presumed to be permanent and unchanging. Consequently, myths are demythologized and nature is historicized. "Allegory is in the realm of thought what ruins are in the realm of things," Benjamin wrote, insisting that the structure of allegory as an artistic procedure is imposed upon the artist by external physical and social conditions as a cognitive imperative, not chosen by the artist as a mere aesthetic preference.[17]

For Benjamin, the ruins of modernity—from buildings blasted apart by war to the detritus of commodity culture—force the recognition not of culture's permanence but of its temporality and transience, just as the decay and disintegration of nature forced baroque poets to confront in their own time the inevitability of catastrophe and death. Like his baroque counterpart, the modern allegorist (the dadaist photomonteur, for example) ceaselessly piles up lifeless, fragmented, arbitrarily exchangeable images "in the unremitting expectation of a miracle," as if the sheer clutter of signs could compensate for the regressive conditions of reception imposed by the depletion of solidly meaningful forms.[18] But the baroque intention "ultimately does not remain faithful to the spectacle of the skeleton [recall Derrida's metaphor], but faithlessly leaps over to the Resurrection."[19] Whereas the baroque allegorist, in his melancholic contemplation, attempted to leave behind the fragmented, transitory realm of failed nature by making the very procedure of objective devaluation in this world the sign of its opposite, that is, of refuge in the eternally redeemed world of the spirit, the modern allegorist confronts a desultory "new nature" whose source of fragmentation is the modern process of production and consumption: "The devaluation of the world of objects within allegory is outdone within the world of objects itself by the commodity."[20] But characteristically the allegorist appropriates these objects and devalues them *a second time*, repeating the process of reification whereby the object is split off from its use value to become a mere signifier of monetary exchange—now in order to dialectically reappropriate the hollowed-out fragments and imbue them with new signification. "The allegorical mind arbitrarily selects from the vast and disordered material that its knowledge has to offer. It tries to match one piece with another to figure out whether they can be combined. This meaning with that image, or that image with this meaning. The result is never predictable since there is no organic mediation between the two."[21] Thus the sequence of appropriation, devaluation, rejuxtaposition, and redistribution of depleted signifiers folds these signifiers, allegorically, into new diagrams and redeems them through the very logic by which they were first devalued. Allegory appears, then, as a displacement of or compensation for a disappearing and irretrievable past, a past foreclosed by the historical and social present.

Like Benjamin's destructive character, Eisenman explicitly and emphatically renounces any attempts at consolation: "Upon close examination these objects reveal that they contain nothing—they are solid, lifeless blocks which seem to have been formerly attached to the context. On the ground is the trace of their movement, their detachment from life. They leave a trace, mark the absence of their former presence: their presence is nothing but an absence."[22] For Eisenman, as Benjamin wrote of Baudelaire, "the century surrounding him that otherwise seems to be flourishing and manifold, assumes the terrible appearance of a desert."[23] Where other architects see in their postmodernism a return to plenitude, in Cannaregio the appropriated, fragmented, and doubly depleted signifiers are nothing if not emblematized iterations of loss in the Benjaminian sense. Indeed, according to Eisenman himself, the series of ghostly voids or holes in the ground that articulate the palpably absent Corbusian origin of the project's grid "embody the emptiness of rationality," "the emptiness of the future," and may be understood as "potential sites for future houses or potential sites for future graves." Now legible only in a highly ambiguous way, since they have been decoded and recoded as something else entirely, these rewritings of modernist ambitions are allegorical diagrams with no content as such—an axiomatic of meaning withdrawn.

It also seems correct to see in this project, involved as it is with the appropriation and semantic nullification of signs, a deliberate and thematic confrontation with the effects of commodification and commercialization of architecture; that is, with the inevitable process in modernity whereby any architectural element loses its use value to become a unit of visual exchange. After all, it is the definitive characteristic of the allegorical object that, once hollowed out, it can be refilled with altogether different content. And indeed by 1978 architectural culture was deluged with various attempts to ballast the free-floating signs of visual exchange by filling them with a dissimulating aura of humanist functionality, cultural continuity, and individual bodily experience, as if such conceptions would restore the symbolic authenticity of thoroughly inauthentic appropriated images and ease the passage of the visual commodity into the private domain of the architectural consumer.

In this sense, the city that Cannaregio's grid traces, or "represents" (though that is no longer quite the right word), is the same city that Denise Scott Brown and Robert Venturi sought to emulate—the city of consumerism, mass media, and multiple publics. But now, according to Eisenman, that city has advanced beyond a threshold of meaningfulness: heterogeneity now becomes utter sameness, and communication is henceforth impossible. For Eisenman the logic of the simulacrum—which of course involves the incorporation and institutionalization of multiplicity in consumer capitalism along with its cognate desires as manifest in Scott Brown and Venturi's postmodernism—in fact precludes representation in any direct way and makes it anachronistic. Speaking of the representational vocation of Venturi's decorated shed, Eisenman writes, "A sign begins to replicate or, in Jean Baudrillard's term, 'simulate,' once the reality it represents is dead. When there is no longer a distinction between representation and reality, when reality is only simulation, then representation loses its a priori source of significance, and it, too, becomes a simulation."[24] What is more, it is this spinning sameness of the simulation that accompanies the particular historical (or posthistorical) impossibility of imagining a future. He continues: "The modern crisis of closure marked the end of the process of moving toward the end. Such crises (or ruptures) in our perception of the continuity of history arise not so much out of a change in our idea of origins or ends than out of the failure of the present (and its

objects) to sustain our expectations about the future."[25] As a result
of this loss of referent and loss of future, the surface semiotics of
Scott Brown and Venturi are, for Eisenman, bits and pieces of
difference that make no difference, further evidence of the perpetual reversion of difference to the same.

All that is left, then, is to jettison their populist ballast so that
nothing but the planimetric surface itself remains, hovering in
midair seared hard and brittle, or pressed into the earth as the
countervailing grids of an archaeological laminate, which, along
with the operations like grafting and scaling that modulate it, is
buried in self-reference. In the name of autonomy and negation,
Eisenman seeks to construct a totality that is exquisitely systematic
and utterly closed and from that totality to produce difference.[26]
But the very isolation is itself historically specific and historically
produced (Eisenman formulates it as a necessary transitional
negation of humanism and anthropomorphism) and as such is
still mediated through a larger cause: the City, if not History itself.
The cities of artificial excavation, not quite representations, are
a form of nonrepresentational mimesis. In their tenacious pursuit
of an architectural system is found a palpable sense of being
locked into the larger structure of society and history, perhaps
even more so than through Scott Brown and Venturi's direct references to the social moment. Indeed Eisenman's pursuit of such
an architectural system is in some ways indistinguishable from
the requirements of the system itself: the relentless, suffocating
sameness, the geological closure, the "end of the beginning, the
end of the end" that must now be recorded. Like a neutron star
whose immense gravity pulls in and distorts matter from surrounding stars, Eisenman's problematic sucks the contradictory
system of autonomy and representation away from Rossi, compresses it while amplifying the heterogeneity-turned-sameness
of Scott Brown and Venturi, and then generalizes the historical
condition of reification, producing process-objects that are traits

and traces of a transitional moment in the great overarching plan that is the spatial imagination. The various gridded laminates of Cannaregio might be thought of as an architectural version of the X-rays emitted from that neutron star, weblike swirls and folds of space whose acoustical approximation would be a dull, slowly pulsating hum and that are only understandable as marks of the forces of reification itself.

"In the conscious act of forgetting, one cannot but remember": in what could be one of the most concise definitions of allegory, Eisenman introduces his 1983 project for the Koch-/Friedrich-strasse Block 5 of Berlin (where Friedrichstrasse intersects the Berlin Wall) as the site of anti-memory.

> *Anti-memory is different from sentimental or nostalgic memory since it neither demands nor seeks a past (nor for that matter a future). But it is not mere forgetting either, because it uses the act of forgetting, the reduction of the former pattern, to arrive at its own structure or order. . . . Anti-memory does not seek or posit progress, makes no claims to a more perfect future or a new order, predicts nothing. It has nothing to do with historical allusion or with the values or functions of particular forms; it instead involves* the making of a place that derives its order from the obscuring of its own recollected past.[27]

Following the same strategies used in Venice, the Berlin project begins with the erasure, reproduction, and superimposition of contingent features of its site. The hypothetically reconstructed eighteenth- and nineteenth-century foundation walls, the Mercator projection, and the implication of the Berlin Wall itself are marked as so many countervailing grids laid onto the site at varying heights developed from the heights of the present streets and the Berlin Wall. All of the buildings proposed for the project can be seen as emerging almost automatically from the initial planimetric strategy. The Koch-/Friedrichstrasse project thus makes explicit what was already implied in Cannaregio: the triadic vocation of the grid as an architectural signifier—at once a diagram of the hypothetical structures of the site (an appropriation of a fictive archaeology), a material support for the building's functions (here little more than an economic division of housing cells, and at Cannaregio even less than that), and a reiterative, self-reflexive structure—a vocation we see tested later in variations at Columbus, Frankfurt, Cincinnati, Long Beach, Paris, Verona, and elsewhere.[28]

Here Eisenman confronts, squarely and architecturally, what Benjamin Buchloh has described as "the essential dilemma" of conceptual art of the mid-1960s: "the conflict between structural specificity and random organization. For the need, on the one hand, for both a systematic reduction and an empirical verification of the perceptual data of a visual structure stands opposed to the desire, on the other hand, to assign a new 'idea' or meaning to an object randomly . . . as though the object were an empty (linguistic) signifier."[29] The random, arbitrary assignment, even invention, of archaeological content in Venice and Berlin opposes the empty, geometrical tautologies of the grid; the historical permeability of concrete architectural form opposes the structure's utter occlusion of any historical reference. And the only available figure of thought that can hold these oppositions of excess and lack together is the *text*—a tissue, textile, or texture of referral and delay in which there is neither beginning nor end, neither a past nor a future. Whether Eisenman's conceptual architecture, with its textualization of every domain of the practice—the site as text, the program as text, the body as text—is a redemptive detour out of reification (the identification of a possible critical vocation for the tissue of fragmented, floating, reified signs) or a postmodern flattening of allegory's material and tragic dimensions is not so much a dilemma of alternatives as a contradiction and a paradox:

the historical paradox of postmodern allegory itself, a paradox that cannot be escaped, a paradox in which Eisenman's work is fully immersed.

Twisting the paradox even tighter, Eisenman's appropriation of already reified material moves to yet a different level in a second operation of Cannaregio. The previously worked out House XIa— itself a formal record of the history of its own formation, comprising nothing more than a series of filmlike stills that trace the steps of devaluation from one state of the object to the next as it sucks itself in, doubles, and burrows in a chthonic-topological transformation (the lower half of the object is fully underground)— now becomes the appropriated object installed at the Venice site. Again, already depleted of its functional, material, and semantic potentials, the house is devalued even more thoroughly, first by its repetition across the site and again by its scaling, that is, the changes in size from that of a house to a series of objects either smaller than a house or larger than a house, each of which, in turn, contains nothing but the shell of the next-smaller object. A kind of diachronic sequence, analogous to Berlin's fictive archaeology, is thereby superinduced on the synchronic structure of the Venetian grid. But the molecular element of the cube—a cube with a smaller cube subtracted from it, which Eisenman calls an "el-cube," a figure awaiting its supplement—operates in opposition with processes of unveiling the formal device, insofar as the el-cube cannot be further broken down by the "decomposition." It is a figure, or better perhaps what Brecht called a *Gestus*—not merely a gesture but a condensation of attitudes, a compression of a complex ideological stance into a singularity. The el-cube as *Gestus* stands in dialectical contradiction to the processes of Cannaregio's *Verfremdungseffekt*.[30] At the same time, the complex repetitions of all the elements of House XIa involve singularities that multiply and reflect one another, such that each of the array of cubes includes difference within itself.

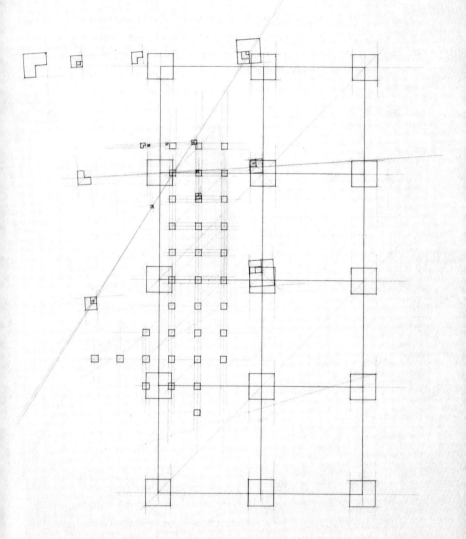

3.4
Peter Eisenman, sketch diagram of two
Cannaregio grids at different scales
in preparation for Choral Works, 1986.
Canadian Centre for Architecture.

And finally, the topological axis of symmetry of the inserted objects is traced as a cut into the ground, a line that connects the two bridges across the canals that delimit the Cannaregio district, reinscribing the territory already defined by the canals. Thus the boundaries of the site and Eisenman's own earlier work, as well as Le Corbusier's project, are all incorporated and grafted into the structure of the new work, now as so many redundant texts that oppose all rooted or solidly signifying usages of presumedly authentic, historical languages (such as Venice's vernacular or Le Corbusier's modernism) in favor of an architectural material, well-formed and precise, that renounces any harmonizing or humanizing refilling in order to move toward the very limits of the signifying practice: an architecture connected not to a pretense of authenticity but to its own abolition; an allegory unto death, half-buried in the Venetian *fondamento*.

This eschatology of forever-deferred ends developed from never-begun beginnings produces a near illegibility or paralysis of reading when, in the Choral Works (1988), Eisenman's extraordinary collaboration with Bernard Tschumi and Jacques Derrida, the Cannaregio project is transported to Paris and superimposed at a different scale onto Tschumi's Parc de la Villette. With the Choral Works, Eisenman pushes the Cannaregio grid as signifier past Venice and Le Corbusier toward some incomprehensible, forever-deferred limit. Here the grid becomes nothing but the signifier of the lack of its own signifying finality, of the fact that it can never express itself fully and indeed has already exceeded itself, collapsing into an illegible singularity. All these ceaseless repetitions and retracings of elements across different sites—the telescoping fall of one element into another that itself duplicates the first and sets up a virtually uncontrollable metonymic series—are by no means inconsistent with the logic of allegory; rather, such obsessive repetition foregrounds the structural or axiomatic aspect of allegory as distinct from the thematic, that is, allegory as a monadic plurality of domains. It is as if the allegorical signifiers carry within themselves the template of the larger allegorical system even as they are only the structural effects of that system. And if later we will want to ask whence comes Eisenman's compulsion to repeat, let us first question its effects.

I have already suggested that the group of artificial excavations is a meditation on the journey of the architectural sign to a visual commodity. But to this it should be added that the repetition and depletion of signs is a successor to the production of defamiliarization and alienation effects mentioned above, a procedure that repeats its object in order to interrogate it, to examine how it came into being, to foreground its arbitrariness, to show, that is, the object as constructed according to the conventional techniques and categories authorized by the discipline itself. The paradigmatic modernist object and its ideology of rationalization and remedial progress toward the future are here grasped not as object but as object symbolized, which is to say object as authorized by the architectural Symbolic. Building on already existing architectures and urban structures but shifting our attention to the ideological devices that normally frame our understanding of form, Cannaregio causes us to reflect directly on architecture's disciplinary presumptions—presumptions about the determinant structure of the site, about architecture's mimetic function, about the ideological status of form. By sliding a hiatus between form and content, the project renders the architectural sign exterior to itself and thus dismantles the ideological self-identity of the routine business of design in order to show just how deeply arbitrary and questionable what everyone takes for granted as obvious, real, and correct actually is. In construing the Cannaregio project in this way, I am insisting that it is by refolding and rescripting material institutions—in the sense that the discipline of architecture itself is an institution—and not merely by manipulating detached forms that Eisenman's work finds its ideological teeth.

But there is more. Eisenman's layering of visual texts—the superimposition of preexisting fabrics, the erasure of their use value, the redoubling of this visual text by his own interventions—and the shift of attention to ideologically motivated disciplinary devices further oblige us to locate the possibility of disciplinary critique in the process of constituting the object in interpretation, that is, in the practice of *reading*. And here we circle back to the notion of performativity. Concretely, this emphasis on performativity implies that the potential of critical action—the critique of the legitimating commercial and educational apparatuses and their classificatory and interpretive procedures—is produced and made available, in a symbolic mode, through new practices of reading propelled by the objects themselves. Through an almost complete "de-skilling" of the architect—an evacuation of craft, taste, and any notion of "good design" as criteria of aesthetic judgment—Eisenman's projects become almost pure ideology effects: registrations of the discursive (not merely formal) features of architecture as an institution, of the very rules of the architectural discourse that determine what can be thought and done.

But to dwell only on the "critical object" as the site of disciplinary critique is to miss the other, related, side of Eisenman's paradoxical procedure, which could be characterized as a kind of euphoria uniting the repetition of discursive codes with the moment in which the subject of the discourse is obliterated. Roland Barthes describes this as an act of reading—or, better, of rescripting—the doxologies of culture: a simultaneous pleasure of repeating what already exists (the enjoyment of cultural or disciplinary identity) and a jouissance of aesthetic disruption.[31] An architecture of pleasure would be a transaction within a bounded inventory of cultural codes, of preexisting elements lifted from the history of the discipline and redeployed. Barthes develops Lacan's notion of jouissance to describe the experience of the abyss that such transactions open up. This is the same "perverse" coupling of affirmation and negation, of reproduction and suspension, that we find in the blank allegory of Eisenman, whose projects are invaded by the ideologies and repetitions of the disciplinary code even as he issues exhortations against them. What else are Eisenman's early houses but empiricist studies of the structural codes of modern architecture and art from Le Corbusier, Terragni, and De Stijl to Robert Morris and Sol LeWitt? In these houses the production of meaning is still a closed process in the sense that we return, again and again, to the most basic cognitive forms of architecture—the cube, the plane, the line, and the point—defamiliarized forms, perhaps, but closed nevertheless. And it is that same doxa that is entered into, opened up, unsettled, and finally blanked out in the profound disenchantment of Venice, where modernist formal logic is systematically reduced and superimposed on a specific site, absorbing the site into its own structure, forcing modernist critique and hope to the sterile condition of tautology. It is here that the modernist aspiration for total self-referentiality coupled with utter randomness is fulfilled, but we must also recognize the heavy price to be paid for that achievement: the complete evacuation of the signified. To read the Cannaregio project for its significance is to read it as a mobile play of signifiers that registers the ideologies of the architectural discipline itself. But the tragedy of history is not thereby transcended, as in classical allegory, nor are its shattered elements refunctionalized, as in modernist allegory. Rather, history is merely displaced by a bleached-out textuality: the anachronic subject falls into nonplace and nontime (Eisenman is explicit about this), into infinite deferral without the conflict of intervening meaning.

The coupling of jouissance and loss strikingly reveals the outer limits of modern subjectivity—the threshold of complete sense liquidation—and, at that borderline, the implacable closure of

Eisenman's signifying economy, whose only (impossible) escape is a kind of death wish.[32] Eisenman's *texte de jouissance* takes a quasi-erotic pleasure in accomplishing the death of its subject in two senses: the dissolution of its content (its discursive subject matter) and of its agent (the author or reader as a subject possessing a disciplinary competence), creating a textual solution wherein the death wish is driven into the very aesthetic reflexivity of his architecture, leaving virtually no material residue to be found within the arid compartments of mirrors constructed by the architecture itself. In contemporary theory the *mise en abyme* has usually been taken as the sign of such aesthetic closure as well as the denial of the historical and sociopolitical contexts that such a mechanism of self-reflection ensures. But it should be underscored again that the infinite redoubling of the sign right up to the edge of the void is only the most extreme register of allegory. Eisenman's allegorical structure enunciates from the start its lost center and establishes as its project to reiterate that loss, infinitely deferring the redemption it promises.

We can now investigate the force behind this death of the subject, but we need to move to yet another level of interpretation to reveal its contours. For what links allegorical repetition to a final, shuddering release, and indeed what lies behind the fusion of repetition, self-immolation, and jouissance, is the Freudian mechanism of *Wiederholungszwang*, or repetition compulsion, which is itself motivated by the death drive—an aggression that is directed inward toward the subject and strives for a kind of subject degree zero through the neutralization of all internal tensions and quantities. The death drive is as fully developed a form of desire as the goal-oriented sexual and life instincts. Indeed, the latter are themselves provoked in characteristic Freudian binary opposition to death's "silent" drive; they are but recuperative responses to the differentiated death drive that continually introduce new desires and tensions into the system.

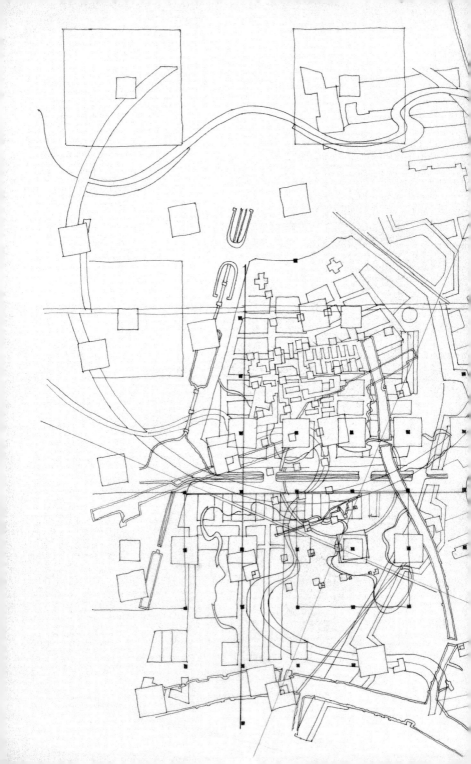

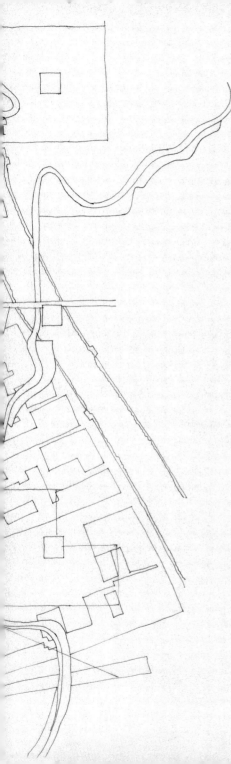

3.5
Peter Eisenman, sketch site plan
showing superimposition of
Cannaregio and La Villette sites at
different scales, 1986. Canadian
Centre for Architecture.

The clinical phenomenon of repetition compulsion was among Freud's principal starting points for his theory of the drive. He observed the syndrome both in the child's tendency to repeat, as in the game of *Fort-Da*, anything found to be effective in diminishing his displeasure during the absence of his mother, and in certain neurotic fixations on traumatic events and the paradoxical regression to unpleasure through the repetition of those events. In *Beyond the Pleasure Principle*, Freud identifies two different forces behind the syndrome of repetition and ascribes both to an instinctual impulse to achieve stasis in the psychic economy and reduce the quantity of stimulation and internal tension to the lowest possible level. On the one hand, there is a seemingly progressive force—*prior to* but not inconsistent with the pleasure principle—by which the subject stages the effects of absence and loss, then works through that material to master unpleasure by means of repetition. On the other hand, there is a force *beyond* the pleasure principle—that is, inconsistent with it—a regressive force that impels the subject to reinstate some previous psychic state (such as a fixation on traumas of war) even when that state yields unpleasure. Giving priority to the regression side of the progression-pleasure/regression-unpleasure dichotomy and combining this with the hypothesis that all repetition is a form of regulatory discharge within the psychic economy, Freud devised a formal definition of instinct: "But how is the predicate of being 'instinctual' related to the compulsion to repeat? . . . *It seems, then, that an instinct is an urge inherent in organic life to restore an earlier state of things* which the living entity has been obliged to abandon under the pressure of external disturbing forces."[33] But if instinct is really a drive to restore an earlier state of things, then a degree zero stage of nonlife appears to be life's ultimate historical aim; the apparatus that strives to nullify all inherent tensions—to divest itself utterly of quantity—is an apparatus that ultimately extinguishes its subject: the death drive. Thus Freud concludes, "Everything living dies for *internal* reasons . . . the aim of all life is death."[34]

Freud's equilibration between the developmental forces of progressive evolution (prior to the pleasure principle) and regressive involution (beyond the pleasure principle) seems to be structurally congruent with Eisenman's conjunction of the pleasure of repeating "a comfortable practice of reading" with the jouissance of imposing "a state of loss." Eisenman's pleasure conforms to the Freudian construction of homeostasis whereby, through repetition as discharge, the psyche seeks to eliminate all quantity. Houses I through VI encode the pleasure of such a reading; they embrace rather than refuse the doxas of the discipline. Reading these projects reproduces within the viewer the pleasure of the paradigms of culture the viewer has internalized—the genre of the single-family house, for example, or the articulation and legibility of forms and procedures still overseen by the symbolic authority of architectural institutions behind the scene. *Fort-Da*: authority is removed, then reconstituted. The subject gravitates to death's void but preserves pleasure by covering over the void with repeated signs. Jouissance is properly beyond the wish for pleasure, transgressing the law of cultural authority with repetition as infinite regress to subjective annihilation. The jouissance of Venice jams the pleasures of reading to train our attention on the shattered origins of the architectural discourse and prevents the architectural text from closing in on a signified; it exploits the elements out of which architectural signs are made, conforming to the Symbolic that circulates around it—but only to pin them to their ultimate inadequacy. For the Symbolic order is also the realm of absence and lack; indeed, of death. If desire depletes its objects, leaving nothing but hollow shells, it is because, at its extreme, desire matches up to nothing but desire itself. And thus Eisenman follows the logic of Freud's repetition compulsion as an avatar of the death drive, where the erotic and thanatotic functions are conjugated in a signifier—repetition—that has as its signified the impossibility of its own signification. "The death drive is only the mask of the symbolic order," Lacan insisted.[35] The death drive is a maximum resolution of the compulsive return to lost origins, to the big Other; and jouissance is but the little death, the orgasmic shudder, experienced when we rehearse that finality.[36]

But if the reader of Freud is hard put to find material evidence of the instinct underlying the compulsion, in Eisenman one faces the fact head on: the repetition compulsion is driven by the windless void of present history and the utter loss of the possibility of signification itself. In his essay "The House of the Dead as the City of Survival," on Rossi's analogous city drawings, Eisenman asserted the exigent program for present-day architecture to be to reckon with post-signification:

> *The problem [we face now is] choosing between an anachronistic continuance of hope and an acceptance of the bare conditions of survival. . . . Incapable of believing in reason, uncertain of the significance of his objects,* man [has lost] his capacity for signifying. . . . *The context which gave ideas and objects their previous significance is gone. . . . The [modernist proposal of the] "death of art" no longer offers a polemical possibility, because the former meaning of art no longer obtains. There is now merely a landscape of objects; new and old are the same; they appear to have meaning but they speak into a void of history. The realization of this void, at once cataclysmic and claustrophobic, demands that past, present, and future be reconfigured.* To have meaning, both objects and life must acknowledge and symbolize this new reality.[37]

We must signify the fact that we can no longer signify; Eisenman generalizes the historical condition of loss and anticipates performative objects able to *sign* their own certificate of death. Reification—the complete penetration of the commodity fetish into the very structure of subjective relations, the complete erasure of all traces of object production—exasperates the desire to *mean* and forces a leap into the void. Eisenman here stages the overall project of the late avant-garde as just such a leap, as the becoming aware of loss—a kind of architectural death drive already latent in the modernism on which Eisenman's work is based.[38] What, then, is his objects' performativity if not the disclosing of the last remaining desiring procedures for signification; and what is his continual appropriation, depletion, and reappropriation of depleted signifiers if not a practical, allegorical use of the compulsion to repeat, an incessant replaying of the reification of signs and the cancellation of the subject, all as a signification that signification is henceforth impossible? "The game is already played, the die already cast," wrote Lacan. "It is already cast, with the following proviso, that we can pick it up again, and throw it anew."[39]

But I am repeating myself, so let me bring this to an end. I have insisted that the reiterability of Eisenman's desiring processes and its consequences—the liquidation of traditional aesthetic experience, the potentiality of disciplinary critique—are played out in the architectural drawing. When Eisenman's project remains within the problematic of representation, then the critical force of the work seems effective. But it is a paradoxical force, for the medium of the critique must be the same abstract and reified material that the critique discloses; and the attempt of these "excavations" to evacuate history, past and future, is itself historically determined. It is just in the nature of the historical moment Eisenman confronts that it is experienced as the bathetic completion of modernist ambitions to graphically refunction abstract signs. Eisenman's architecture is accurate and legitimate but perhaps also, in its representation of a culture dispossessed of meaning, obedient.

When the drawings are translated into built works, as in the housing block in Koch-/Friedrichstrasse, for example, Eisenman's glass beads of perfect repetition are thrown against the hard floor of building practice. A contradiction emerges that he was able to avoid in the never-to-be-built Cannaregio project: the functionalization of the dysfunctional diagram and the aestheticization of the conceptual sign. Eisenman's response is conservative. It derives from a reluctance to accept the complete disintegration of the aesthetic object, even after the radically altered historical circumstances that affect the conditions of architectural production and reception were recognized in Cannaregio and such a disintegration was first enunciated. The anti-aesthetic signifiers now reappear in a kind of aesthetic atavism, attempting (one last time) to recoup investments in meaning already liquidated, refusing the destiny Eisenman himself had already predicted. Yet it is just this performative contradiction (the refused destiny, its cynical truth claim) that gives the built work its power: it repeats the objective conditions under which any work of architecture in the present must be produced—the constant struggle against the two equally intolerable poles of mere obedient service to existing institutions and mere aesthetic voluntarism. Before hoping to surpass the contradiction, Eisenman must perforce repeat it. Such unresolved antagonisms of reality reappear in architectural form.

Plate 1
Aldo Rossi and Gianni Braghieri,
Cemetery of San Cataldo, Modena,
1971, aerial perspective. Courtesy
Fondazione Aldo Rossi.

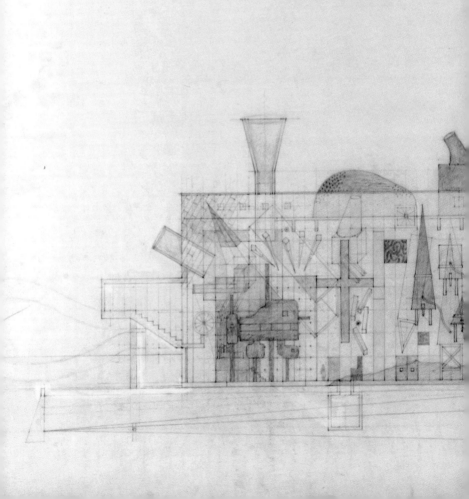

Plate 2
John Hejduk, Cathedral, 1996,
X-ray drawing. Canadian Centre
for Architecture.

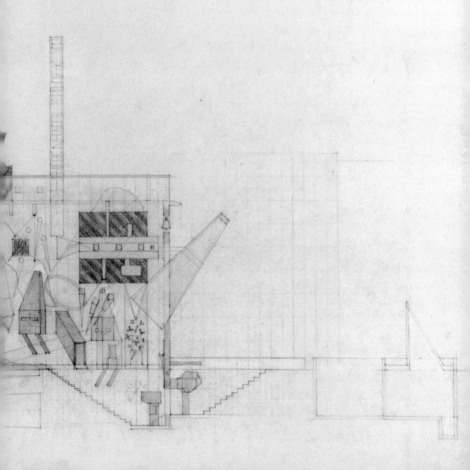

Plate 3
John Hejduk, Sanctuary 1 (1-02)
(1 of 17 parts), 1999–2000.
The Menil Collection.

Plate 4
John Hejduk, Enclosure 9
(1 of 32 parts), 2000.
The Menil Collection.

Plate 5
Aldo Rossi, project for Fagnano
Olona school, plan, 1972.
Courtesy Fondazione Aldo Rossi.

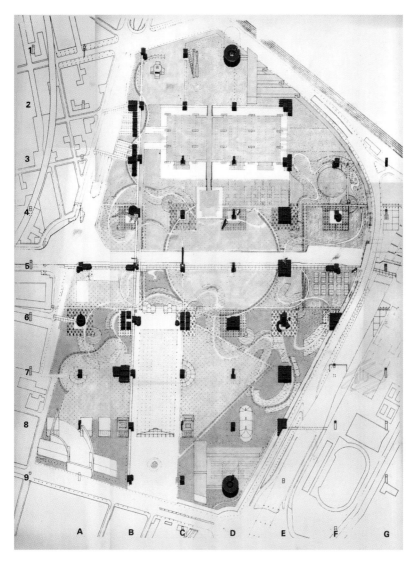

Plate 6
Bernard Tschumi, Parc de la Villette,
1982, plan. Courtesy of the architect.

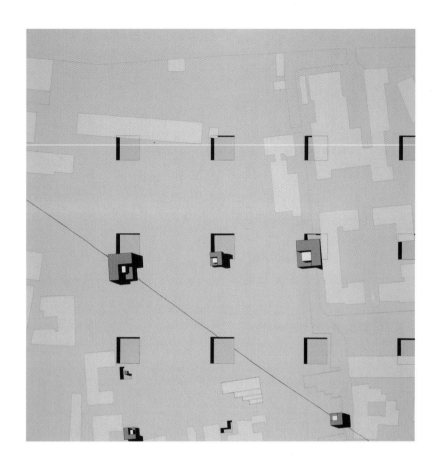

Plate 7
Peter Eisenman, project for
Cannaregio, 1978, plan.
Canadian Centre for Architecture.

YALE UNIVERSITY
NEW HAVEN · CONNECTICUT · 06520

DEPARTMENT OF COMPARATIVE LITERATURE
1113 BINGHAM HALL

très solide ressemblerait à la fois à une trame, à un crible ou une grille (GRID) et à un instrument de musique à corde (CHORD).
(piano, harpe, lyre?)

En tant que grille, grid, etc., il aurait un certain rapport avec le filtre interprétatif et sélectif qui aurait permis de lire et de cribler les 3 sites et les 3 couches (PDE, BT, LV), etc. En tant qu'instrument à corde il figurerait le choral et choral work. Je crois que rien ne devrait être inscrit sur cette sculpture, à moins que, peut-être, quelques le titre et une signature n'y figurent quelque part (choral work, by ... -1986 ...) - A discuter, entre autres choses.

3.6

Jacques Derrida, letter to Peter Eisenman with sketch proposal for an intervention in Bernard Tschumi's project for La Villette, May 30, 1986. Courtesy Marguerite Derrida. **"And more than grille, grid, etc., it will have a certain rapport with a selective and interpretive filter, telescope, or photographic filter and aerial view, which allows the reading and the screening (sifting?) of the three sites, the three layers (PDE, BT, LV)."**

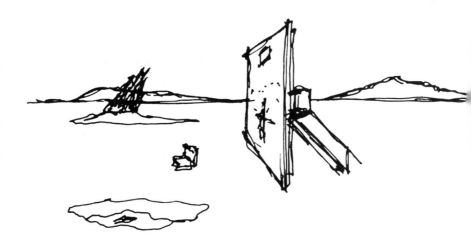

ENCOUNTER

Form for the late avant-garde appears as a fatedness—an inhuman force that enables and organizes architectural concepts while imposing itself as a blockage to any different future experiences. Expression, meanwhile, demands interaction among situation, viewer, and the larger culture out of which architecture arises; it requires reorganizing shapes, geometries, scenes, and materials into affective units. To achieve these things, expression needs to press the death instinct into its service, yielding to the mandate of absence and repetition to produce perceptions of difference—as something that happens to us, that interrupts, that throws us out of joint. This dialectic is an originary structural necessity that lies at the heart of architectural practice, not an affliction from outside. It is, in fact, the property of architectural desire itself, which lies on the borderline between the bleached-out abstractions of formalism (pure desire is "the pure and simple desire of death as such")[1] and the aesthetic expressions we as individuals mistakenly believe to have been made for us alone.

This same dialectic is found in the work of the entire late avant-garde. Thus the repetition of form already detectable in Rossi's projects and intensified in Eisenman's persists in Hejduk's work, but now as encounter, situation, and event. Here we confront an architecture not, like Eisenman's, indifferent to sensuous experience, but rather decidedly animated and personified even if not quite human. Like the animals in a fable that speak with human voices, Hejduk's objects seem, impossibly, to be aware of us, to address us. And yet we see not the gratifying reflection of ourselves we had hoped for but another thing looking back at us, watching us, placing us. The way in which Hejduk's architecture encounters its viewer, the way in which the encounter takes place or, better, is a taking *of* place, and, more specifically, the way in which the architectural form *wall* is constructed as the expressive apparatus that enables or enacts that taking of place is a fundamental theme—*the* fundamental theme—in Hejduk's entire body of work. Here I chart the development of that theme.

In an early (1963) but often-repeated explication of the Diamond Houses (the series of carefully calibrated and measured formal transformations, executed between 1963 and 1967, that owe much to Piet Mondrian, Le Corbusier, and Mies van der Rohe), Hejduk constructs a diagram of the history of architectural space, declaring the paradigmatic space of the present to be the compression onto a vertical two-dimensional surface of the space generated by the two legs of a right angle. The logic goes something like this: If the primitive condition of architecture is the square, the square is nevertheless generated as the isometric projection of a diamond, making the diamond paradoxically prior to, or more primitive than, the square. Yet if the diamond is understood perceptually as the plan diagram of an architectural space rather than as a two-dimensional graphic shape, then the most fundamental percept of the space of the diamond is another square now locked into the vertical plane, one that results from collapsing the two legs of the diamond's right angle, projected as vertical planes or walls, onto a picture plane. In other words, the diamond returns to the square in the event of its perception. This is true whether the viewer is outside the diamond plan, with the protruding exterior corner reduced to an invisible line on the perceptual plane, or inside the plan, with the corner now retreating, but with no perceivable difference.

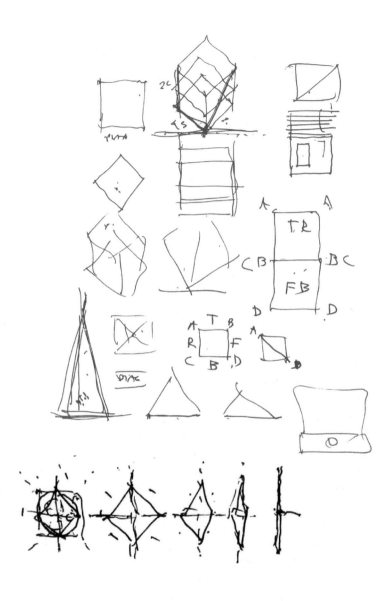

4.1
John Hejduk, Diamond Museum C,
c. 1962. Explanatory sketches.

What is more, this compression of deep space onto a flat eleva-tional surface is homologous with both the picture plane onto which the perspectival space of the Renaissance is projected—Alberti's famous vertical membrane on which traces of the lines of vision are inscribed—and the anti-Albertian canvas of the cubist still life (think of the table of the still life tilted up verti-cally), in which perspective's beginning and end, the vanishing point, is always absent. Developing the classicist-modernist axioms of flatness versus depth and opacity versus transparency, Hejduk understands this percept—the image of the flattening or collapsing of deep space onto the square vertical plane—as at once the most basic element of any architecture (the summation of the history of architectural space to date) and a historically specific phenomenon. For the percept itself is located on the crease in time between the past and the future. "It's a beautiful distance," he declares of the space and time seen backward and forward from this plane. "As you go back into space it gets into deeper perspective, it gets less clear and you can never really complete it, because that's the unknown, it isn't fixed. So it gets darker. As you get closer to the present, it's clearer. On the plane of the present is that horizontal armature, which is the hypotenuse; you just speculate on futures."[2] The diagram at the bottom of a series of sketches for the Diamond Houses lecture is Hejduk's shorthand notation for the coming into being of this space-time apparatus. It is for him the fundamental mechanism of expression by which architecture pushes its most basic logic, its genetic code, out into the realm of the visible. And that becoming—the sequence of events in which deep space and past time is collapsed onto a vertical surface—subtends the entire trajectory of Hejduk's career.

In Kantian vocabulary, *form* arises when a multiplicity of sen-sations are connected in agreement with one another, resulting in a perceptual unity that is not covered by and cannot be subsumed under a conceptual unity. (It is just the extent to which aesthetic judgments of taste resist conceptual analysis while still claiming universal validity that makes them the privileged moments of the *Critique of Judgment*.) Such a *perceptum*, as Kant called this form, cannot be attributed to an object itself. Rather, it can be perceived only in the singularity of the event addressed by aesthetic judgment. It is as if Hejduk, at this point in his career, has assimilated the Kantian machinery of singular appearances and events and constructed his own moment of Kantian form, for it is quite clear that the diamond percept is an event in this sense, what Hejduk called the "moment of the hypotenuse."

4.2
John Hejduk, Wall House, sketch, c. 1968. Canadian Centre for Architecture.

The research of the Diamond House and its perceptual screen made possible the "discovery" of the Wall House (for it is as if it had always been there in the architectural unconscious waiting for an event to trigger its *Nachträglichkeit*), about which Hejduk wrote, "In order to have a-priori principles meaningful, and to give up and put forth organic revelations, there had to be a given form."[3] The Wall House is Hejduk's architectural still life of biomorphic shapes and fragments of geometric objects now hovering in elevation in front of an actual thin, taut wall plane (the form), rather than being deployed back, deep in plan, behind a perceptual plane as in the Diamond Houses.[4] "The wall represents the same condition of the 'moment of the hypotenuse' in the Diamond houses—it's the moment of greatest repose, and at the same time the greatest tension. It is a moment of passage. The wall heightens that sense of passage, and by the same token, its thinness heightens the sense of it being just a momentary condition . . . what I call the moment of the 'present.'"[5] One thinks of Picasso's still life *The Architect's Table* (1912)—its shifting layers and transparencies, its attempt to make a new pictorial order out of perception itself, but always through the conventions and the procedures of painting. But more important for Hejduk is Georges Braque's *Studio III*, in which a bird seems to fly through a wall, a painting that Hejduk obsessed over because in it the wall is not an object as such but rather a singular figure that nevertheless possesses a universality, directing and determining how that object appears at a certain time and place. The wall must constantly transform and deform itself into its other; it must direct discrepancies to its unity; it must, for example, have a bird fly through it. The wall brings forth the bird as the bird brings forth the wall in a singular assemblage, wall-becoming-bird. Hejduk's Wall House is the architect's version of the cubist dream of bringing into being a new order, with all its contradictions, with all its totalizing tendencies, and with all its world-making ambitions.

A dimension of the figural is already present in the Wall House—not of clichéd images or recycled meanings; rather, it is a dimension of gesture and referral that opens up a sense of a world outside the purely syntactical organizations whose domain, it has been assumed, encloses the early experiments of both Hejduk and Eisenman (recall that the Wall Houses were first presented with Eisenman's early house projects as having common purpose).[6] It is apparent that every element of the Wall House comes from the formal repertoire of Le Corbusier (think especially of Villa La Roche and the blank wall at the monastery of La Tourette), and yet our encounter with the Wall House is an experience unassimilable within Corbusian codes. We find ourselves forced to resort to a language of psychological and phenomenal forces, of emotions and affections, of an unencoded or preencoded morphology that works first upon sensation before it quickly collapses back into known fact—Cézanne's "airy, colored logic suddenly ousting somber, stubborn geometry" (and we know of Hejduk's obsession with Cézanne).[7] I think this excess comes partly from an ambiguity about occupation: Do we inhabit the house (only one person at a time, it seems), or does it inhabit an environment of its own creation, projected out of its claim to emplacement, and necessarily independent? None of the Wall House variants were designed for actual sites, yet they take their place. The Wall House is an inhabitable threshold between outside and inside, back and front, *Fort-Da*: a conceptual, imagined "gone" and an embodied, perceived "here." That is, it exists in percept and memory as much as in reality, virtually more than actually (hence disturbing phenomenological notions of *corps vécu*), constituting what Hejduk called "moments of passage" and "a coming to pass," points of contact between the solace and security of the internal and eternal and the uncertainties of the external and now.

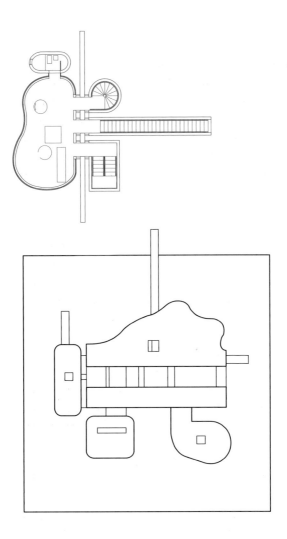

4.3
John Hejduk, Wall House 3, 1974 elevation
and plan. "If the painter could, by a single
transformation, take a three-dimensional still
life and paint it on a canvas into a *natura
morta,* could it be possible for the architect to
take the *natura morta* of a painting and, by a
single transformation, build it into a still life?"

At the same time, the Wall House makes explicit another condition of figure that was only implied in the Diamond Houses, but will be explored in subsequent projects. The viewing subject of architecture is not just the observer of an object focused as an image and arrayed before him or her on the plane of perception. Rather, the subject is also produced by the architecture, in the moment of encounter, inasmuch as the architecture—or better, the architectural big Other operating behind the scene of encounter—exerts a defining, identifying force back on the subject, and in the same vertical plane, so to speak. Architecture is the point of subjectification from which the viewer's subject position emerges. As noted, Hejduk understands the elevational surface, together with its temporal dimension, as the topos of the cultural reserve of spatial organizations, of which each moment of architectural experience is just one instance. All of architecture's latent possibilities, the entire architectural language, lie waiting in accumulated layers just behind the plane. "It's physical by memory," he says of this plane at one point. His elevational surface— the Wall as a signifying apparatus—contains all the sedimented conventions of the discipline, the codes of architecture built up over centuries from Alberti to Le Corbusier and Mies (shadowed by Picasso and Braque), overlaid with qualifications and values, shot through with the ideals and ideologies of past generations. For Hejduk, the Wall is thus a site of desiring transactions analogous to Rossi's typological Imaginary. But whereas Rossi's system is primarily concerned with the processes of the object, Hejduk's is concerned more with the event of subject formation. It is "all-encompassing," he says of the Wall, "it's an expanding universe. It's emanating from a center; it's an explosive center." And you are not just looking at it: "you are in it," he insists. "You become an element of an internal system of organisms."[8]

The Wall pushes back at the looker. Walter Benjamin noticed this phenomenon of reciprocal viewing and linked it to the presence of aura:

> [What was] felt to be inhuman, one might even say deadly, in daguerreotypy was the (prolonged) looking into the camera, since the camera records our likeness without returning our gaze. But looking at someone carries the implicit expectation that our look will be returned by the object of our gaze. Where this expectation is met . . . , there is an experience of the aura to the fullest extent. . . . Experience of aura thus rests on the transposition of a response common in human relationships to the relations between the inanimate or natural object and [the person] . . . . To perceive the aura of an object we look at means to invest it with the ability to look at us in turn. This experience corresponds to the data of the mémoire involontaire.[9]

But Hejduk's Wall focuses that involuntary memory—the vaporous memory of architecture's own history—in the present instance of embodied vision. The corporeal-temporal dimension of the plane of encounter keeps what might otherwise freeze into a final reified image from ever fixing itself. Its mnemonics are emergent rather than residual, and any memories produced must be constantly renegotiated.

Indeed, in this respect Hejduk's own comments on the Wall apparatus are akin to the famous contemporaneous story (1964) by Lacan, who writes of seeing a sardine can floating on the sea, glittering in the sun, and looking back at him, it seems, situating him, pinning him to a fundamental lack in his own self and to his own decentered moment. The encounter led Lacan to his theory of the double articulation of the subject as both viewer of the object and under the regard of the object, pictured by its "gaze." Lacan specifies that only through a visual engagement with a virtual counterpart, in a mirror or on a screen, can we acquire identity. He diagrams this in a way very similar to Hejduk's spatial apparatus. On the one hand is the perspectival cone of the Renaissance, the *trompe-l'oeil* that produces and organizes the image for us on the transparent picture plane. On the other hand is an opposite cone that emanates from the object itself, like a projected light coming at us (like the light from the sardine can), which we cannot control and which Lacan calls the "gaze." In this projected light, coinciding with the plane of the image, is an interrupting screen, opaque rather than transparent. Lacan calls it the *dompte-regard*, a membrane or blotter that subdues or mediates the gaze for us and helps us to negotiate its blinding light. Lacan calls the coincidence of the two planes the "image-screen" or the "mask," and it is this that both determines what can and cannot be seen and how it is seen and helps us to manage what is seen by giving us an Imaginary-Symbolic system with which to represent things to ourselves and ourselves to others. "Man, in effect, knows how to play with the mask as that beyond which there is the gaze," Lacan states. "The screen is here the locus of mediation."[10] Hejduk's image-screen, with its similar dialectic

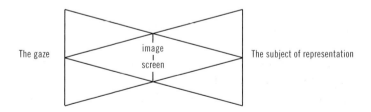

The gaze — image / screen — The subject of representation

4.4
Jacques Lacan, diagram of the gaze. From *The Four Fundamental Concepts of Psycho-Analysis*.

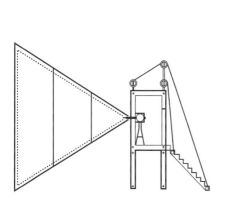

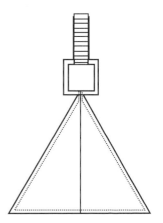

4.5
John Hejduk, Identity Card Man, from
the Victims series, 1986. **"Collects
identity card / photographs card /
Projects film of card onto screen /
Once— / destroys negative / explicit
faith in memories / hallucination /
of signatures."**

of flatness and depth, opacity and transparency—his Mask of Medusa—is his Wall. The Wall traces Architecture's gaze; we are placed before the Wall by Architecture's gaze. For Hejduk as for Lacan, the image-screen is an apparatus of the Imaginary/ Symbolic necessary for our social and cultural existence—a historically generated repertoire of images and codes through which we as social subjects are constructed in something like an architectural mirror stage (can it be a mere coincidence that one side of Hejduk's wall is a mirror?) by forces of architectural desire.[11]

The reading of Hejduk's architecture as a machinery of subject construction finds a confirmation of stunning precision in one of the units from the Victims series of 1986, the Identity Card Man, described as follows:

> *Collects identity card*
> *photographs card*
> *Projects film of card onto screen*
> *Once—*
> *destroys negative*
> *explicit faith in memories*
> *hallucination*
> *of signatures*[12]

The subject's identity is photo-graphed, inscribed by light; it is projected onto a screen; the subject is signed as a hallucination, a *méconnaissance*; on the membrane of the Imaginary, populated by *objets petite a*, he is but a mnemonic stain.

But this project of 1986 takes us too far ahead. Late in 1973 Hejduk traveled to Zurich for an exhibition of his and Aldo Rossi's work at the Eidgenössische Technische Hochschule, where Rossi was teaching.[13] There, for the first time, he saw Rossi's provocative and haunting drawings for the residences at Gallaratese (1970), the school at Fagnano Olona (1972), and the City Hall for Muggiò

(1972). He also saw the Cemetery of San Cataldo at Modena (1971). The encounter with Rossi made a crease in Hejduk's career, which between 1973 and 1975 would fold back on itself in a reexamination of accomplishments to date and reconsideration of his work's trajectory in the light of what he saw in Zurich. What struck Hejduk in Rossi's work was not simply a typology of reduced forms comparable to Hejduk's own (as a contemporaneous critic aptly described them, "a few finished elements that are geometrically precise, insisted on in an almost obsessional manner, fixed in time and continuously refined");[14] it was, rather, the *discrepancy* between Rossi's stated intent to subsume all of the architectural Imaginary into a finite, iterable categorization of types and the dimension of Rossi's work that eludes and exceeds such enclosure. Hejduk saw the heterogeneities and singularities that geometry cannot hold. In the Modena project Hejduk noticed, for example, the estrangements and *détournements* from Ledoux's ideal city of Chaux, Boullée's cenotaph, and Piranesi's Campo Marzio; the latent references to the *Sachlichkeit* of Hilberseimer and Loos, even to Hannes Meyer's little-known 1923 cemetery project; and also allusions to the paintings of de Chirico, Sironi, and Morandi, the films of Fellini and Visconti, and the novels of Raymond Chandler and Raymond Roussel. Hejduk heard the multimedia murmur behind Rossi's silence. The daemons of the analogous city were whispering to him. And he wondered about unleashing all that Rossi had suppressed.

The Wall House was Hejduk's available device of temporal, narrative potential and radical figuration—a form that directs an event. Together these two features of narrative and figure structure the desiring field that will become his answer to Rossi's analogous city. Hejduk's preliminary response (in what at first seems a surprisingly tentative staking out of new territory) was the Cemetery for the Ashes of Thought (1975), in which he breathed life into Wall House 3 (1974), reanimating it to stand as sentinel across a lagoon from the old Mulino Stucky building in Venice ("The little house was colored overlooking the monochromatic, systemic, European world").[15] Other than the Wall House and the mill, the proposal is for nothing more than a columbarium defined by low walls with holes ("holes," not niches or urns) holding containers with ashes and plaques with the titles and authors of canonic Western literature. An existing abandoned mill, a house designed a year earlier, walls with holes—almost nothing. And yet Hejduk himself sees this project as a turning point in his work—"a commentary not only on commentary but of my essential belief in the reductive attitude"—which suggests that the radical lack we feel with regard to this project is quite fundamental.[16] The Cemetery for the Ashes of Thought precisely constructs an elementary diagram of desire, according to which the unavailability or interdiction of a desired object—in this case the thought that is both dematerialized and symbolized in the ashes—becomes an attracting void of enormous significance. The potter shapes the void that produces the prospect of fullness. Lacan cites Heidegger regarding the primordial signifier that creates the void: "The existence of the emptiness at the center of the real that is called the Thing, this emptiness as represented in the representation presents itself as a *nihil*, as nothing."[17]

The Thing (*Ding*), while not a major concept in Freud's own work, is fundamental in Lacan (beginning in Seminar VII).[18] Freud introduces the Thing in the "Judging and Remembering" section of the 1895 "Project for a Scientific Psychology" (not published until 1950), where he analyzes the subjective constitution of the knowledge of reality, focusing on the "primary perceptive complex," or *Nebenmensch* complex, the primary subject-object encounter. In one of his most Kantian moments, Freud argues that the work of judgment aims at a state of identity between drive and object; that the *Nebenmensch* complex is resolved when cognition (*Erkennen*) reduces the other to the same

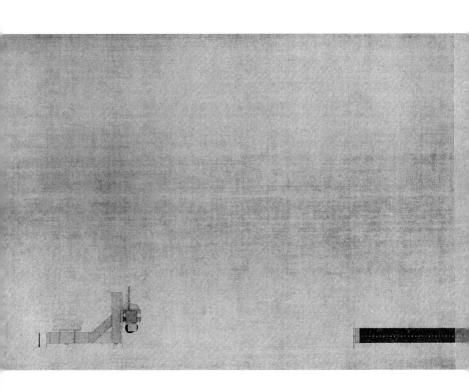

4.6
John Hejduk, Cemetery for the
Ashes of Thought, 1975, elevation
showing Mulino Stucky building
to the right and Wall House 3 in the
lagoon to the left.

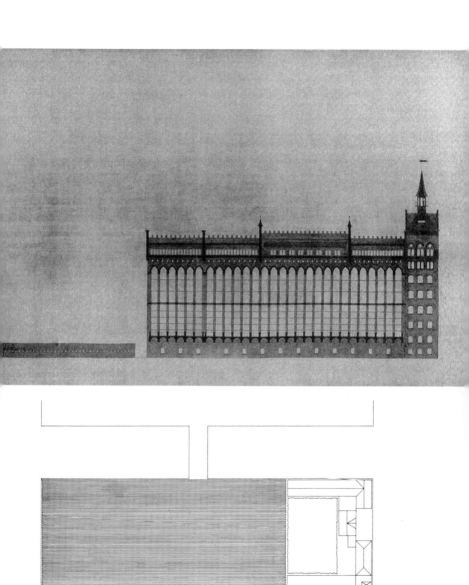

"Cemetery of the ashes of thought"
"Cimetero per gli ceneri dei pensieri"

4.7
John Hejduk, Cemetery for the
Ashes of Thought, 1975,
aerial perspective sketch showing
the cemetery on the Giudecca.
Canadian Centre for Architecture.

in the event of judgment. The child's ability to cognize, then, depends on the child's relationship to the *Nebenmensch*—"fellow human-being" in the Standard Edition translation, "the first satisfying object" according to Freud, which is to say the mother in the first instance, but the mother seen in a startlingly different frame, for the *Nebenmensch* is also a threat and an enemy, "das erste feindliche Objekt." "Proximate creature" may be a better approximation, for from the start there is a disturbance in this relationship, which splits the *Nebenmensch* into "two components, of which one makes an impression by its constant structure and stays together as a *thing* [*als Ding*], while the other can be understood by the activity of memory—that is, can be traced back to information from [the subject's] own body."[19] Lacan glosses the two components of the *Nebenmensch* complex, first, as *das Ding*, the part that "remains together as a thing" but alien ("*entfremdet*, something strange to me, although it is at the heart of me"); and second, as *Vorstellungen*, the system of representations or signifiers through which the *Nebenmensch* can be *remembered*. Lacan stresses vigorously that this particular nameless object (or frame of an object, an object thus set up), *das Ding*, is the primary object on which is grounded all possible subject-object relations and, equally, the empty site that remains when entry into the Symbolic is complete. "*Das Ding* is at the center only in the sense that it is excluded. That is to say, in reality *das Ding* has to be posited as exterior, as the pre-historic Other that is impossible to forget."[20] It is crucially important for us that Lacan's meditation on *das Ding* in Seminar VII is constitutively involved with his most sustained discussion of aesthetics. To encounter the aesthetic object is to experience the uncanny proximity of the exterior in the most interior, which is nothing less than a bit of the Real at the very center of Symbolic order. Furthermore, Lacan uses architecture as his primary example of this encounter, citing the ancient temple as "a construction around emptiness that designates the place of the Thing."[21] He might just as well have cited Hejduk's cemetery.

In the Cemetery for the Ashes of Thought, the *Ding* component of Lacan's split encounter is represented (the Thing is something "only a representation can represent") by the missing texts—the Thought, the central object of Western culture that cannot be signified even as it is the event horizon of all signification, that must be continually "refound" but is "never there in the first place to be lost," in comparison with which all other objects will be more unsatisfactory substitutes.[22] The Thing recalls us to trauma; Freud says that it announces itself in a scream (*wenn es schreit*) that recalls me to my own screaming (and the barbarism of Nazi book burnings echoes across the Giudecca). A prelinguistic affect, it can present itself only to the extent that it becomes unspoken word, ashes of thought; otherwise, it resists altogether any attempt at comprehension, since the codes for its cognition simply do not exist. Wall House 3, *Nebenmensch*—the proximate character, beside but apart—thus becomes an integral part of this template, for the Wall House gives up its meaning as *Vorstellungen*, through memory, as we have seen. It remains an object outside that nevertheless creates that outside, where it too will thus appear alien, ungraspable, even cruel, insofar as it can be actualized only by memories sometimes painful. For Hejduk, it is not simply the loss of some original Architecture that creates a desire to recover it. Rather, it is the desire to fill the emptiness or void at the core of the architectural Symbolic that produces (retrospectively, from the outside in, as it were) the very object-cause of desire itself—Architecture, not in actuality but in effect. If this is not the lesson of the Cemetery for the Ashes of Thought, then it holds none.

Since 1974 Venice has preoccupied the nature of my work. It is a forum of my inner arguments. The thoughts have to do with Europe and America; abstraction and historicism;

the individual and the collective; freedom and totalitari-
anism; the colors black, white, grey; silence and speech;
the literal and the ambiguous; narrative and poetry; the
observer and the observed. . . . I suspect in these past
four years my architecture has moved from the "Archi-
tecture of Optimism" to what I call the "Architecture of
Pessimism."[23]

This statement is from the text accompanying Thirteen Watch-
towers of Cannaregio (1979)—a project that makes up a trilogy,
with Silent Witnesses (1976) and the Cemetery for the Ashes of
Thought, around the unassimilable architectural Thing. It is as
precise an account as any of Hejduk's work around 1979, and it
can stand as a list of his concerns as his attention moves from the
City trilogy outward in a series of projects called the "masques."
In the tradition of the Italian *maschera* and the festival architecture of Inigo Jones, the masques propose various interacting
human inhabitants and architectural characters—architectural
troubadours, vagabonds, and itinerants—that travel in caravans
from city to city (Berlin, Vladivostok, Lancaster, Hanover), twisting
the mundane urbanism of their sites into carnivalesque narrative
encounters. The taking of place is the masques' very mode of
being. More daringly than the Wall House or the Cemetery, the
masques open a lens onto architecture's otherness, as Hejduk
begins to catalog the multiple, idiosyncratic recodings of architectural elements: his menagerie of angels, animals, martyrs, and
machines; his stylistic preference for basic geometric forms and
elemental biomorphism (buildings that seem to have hair, beaks,
eyes, and legs), combined with typological variations on theaters,
periscopes, funnels, traps, chapels, and labyrinths; his thematic
explorations of falls from grace, itinerancy, passage, and transformation; and his belief in architecture as sanctuary—for art,
culture, the enduring rituals that mark us as human, and for

the human spirit itself—though often sanctuary is developed in darker ways too, for these temporary villages and their characters also refer to the walled ghettos and golems of European cities and the westward colonizing caravans of North America.

In the masques, the subject-object distinction, already disturbed in the Wall Houses and Cemetery, is utterly collapsed. After all, anything that can stand upright on legs and look at you (as many of the units from the masques do) can lay claim to a more complex mode of being than a mere aesthetic object. Moreover, the inhabitants of Hejduk's chosen cities are deterritorialized into their vocations (the workers, the dwellers, the butter women, the bank key man, for example). Buildings likewise are interchangeable pieces of mechanical equipment, wheels and pulleys that grind and creak, that are always on the move; and the city itself becomes a smooth space of surrealist ambiance and shifting moods that, like the Wall, registers past events and projects possible future ones. Hejduk's masques and their urban settings seem to reciprocally presuppose one another, even if they must remain quite independent and even contradictory. We are in the realm of the "as if," for nothing is typical (typological) now; everything is only *like* something else.

In his cities of artificial excavation Eisenman strives to find an architecture of pure trace, which effaces itself before the theory, the critique, and the thought it is asked to convey. We might call this a philosophical paradigm for architecture. By way of this comparison, Hejduk's model is a literary one, which tends toward the opposite direction—toward an accumulation of different types of discourses or references or items in all their messy opacity and refractivity (one thinks of Borges's impossible Chinese taxonomy of animals—"those that belong to the Emperor, embalmed ones, those that are trained, suckling pigs, mermaids, fabulous ones, . . ."—incompatible categories compressed onto the same plane). Or Rossi. His City, we saw, has an afterward—a persistence that enacts different uses, perceptual systems, and understandings of its enduring types—but also a before—a built-in possibility of being repeated. On this comparison, Hejduk introduces a more radical dimension of heterogeneity into the construction of repetition. Rossi instructs us that a type never presents itself only once; in order to be typological, an element must be recognizably the same over time, must be comparable with earlier and later instances of itself. But there is something in Hejduk's repetitions that cannot be wholly absorbed into the identification of the same. There is something that stalls, arrests, something that won't go through: it remains, it bothers, it haunts. Derrida, to return to his classic essay on repetition, calls this something *le reste*, translated as "remainder" but also as "the rest"—all that is differential to self-sameness. In Lacanian terminology, the objects are "extimate"; *das Ding*, the void of the Cemetery, is now contained within the most intimate encounters with the objects[24]—the exorbitant remainder that cannot be managed by symbolization.

We perceive the exorbitance of the masques in part as ambiance, mood, affect—as narrative systems of time and space that produce a distinctive phenomenal "feel" of places we may have actually visited but that remain intractably alien. The masques, perhaps like no other architecture, insist that we ponder certain questions: What is the relation of subjective action to its objective context? Does the context produce events, or is it mere background? Is a building an environment or an individual? Are subjects fixed, or are they replaceable, exchangeable, momentary? Is it possible for events to be repeated or reversed? Is time open to multiple interpretations, or is it scripted in advance? Is there a concept of public time and space, of the collective as opposed to the private narrative? Indeed, are Hejduk's narratives of troupes and carnivals so private and so out of time and place, anachronic and anatopic, that they overspin what may count for a proper and plausible yarn?

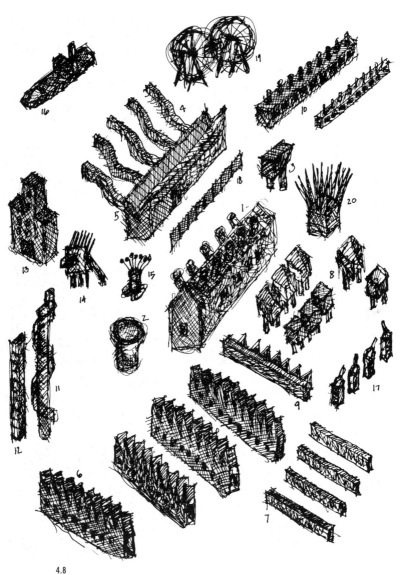

4.8
John Hejduk, Berlin Masque,
1981, characters.

(24) ARBITRATION HALL

SEE: DEFINITION:
FOR THE ARBITRATION OF
DIFFERENCES. THIS HALL
CAN BE CONSIDERED THE
COUNTER-POINT TO THE
MASQUE, ONE INVOLVED
WITH THE JUDICIAL THE
OTHER WITH A SILENT
RITUAL.
THE STRUCTURE IS CONSTRUCTED
OF REINFORCED CONCRETE
(FLOOR SLAB) AND STEEL,
METAL CLAD. THE MEDUSA
LIKE LIGHT-WELLS (OPEN TO
THE WEATHER) LET IN LIGHT
AND ACT AS A VENTING
   A SPECIFIC SET OF
INTERIOR ELEMENTS ARE
CONSTRUCTED OF HARD WOODS
AND ARE CAREFULLY FINISHED
IN BEES WAX.

LOCATION: NEAR CROSS OVER-BRIDGE

(15)

TO THE NORTH IS THE SILENT
AUDIENCE; TO THE EAST THE
SUB-MASQUE FOR A SINGLE
MALE INHABITANT (SELECTED
BY THE CITY OF BERLIN); TO
THE WEST A SINGLE FEMALE
INHABITANT (SELECTED BY
THE CITY OF BERLIN); AND
TO THE SOUTH OUTSIDE IS A
STEEL FRAME ELEMENT
WHICH SUPPORTS FLOOD LIGHTS
AND LOUD SPEAKERS, A SUPPORT
SYSTEM FOR LIGHT (THE SUN
WORKS IN THE DAY); THIS
SYSTEM OPERATES AT NIGHT.
FINALLY, AN ENTRY-EXIT TO
THE EAST METAL FUNNEL
(PAST); TO THE WEST AN
ENTRY-EXIT: A MEDUSA FUNNELS
THE MALE ELEMENT BEING IN
THE PAST LOOKING TOWARDS THE
FUTURE; THE FEMALE ELEMENT
IN THE FUTURE LOOKING BACK
AT THE PAST.

CONTINUE...

(26) UNITS (A) & (B) [HOUSING]

THE CRUX

THE SINGLE INDIVIDUALS
HOUSING NEEDS ARE THE LAST
TO BE CONSIDERED. THAT IS
THE SINGLE FEMALE, SINGLE
MALE, FROM THE AGE GROUP
12 TO 80. THE SINGLE PERSON
WHO WISHES TO REMAIN SINGLE
AND PRIVATE. WHO WISHES
TO INHABIT HER OR HIS OWN
PLACE, THAT IS TO LIVE ALONE
NOT NECESSARILY TO BE A
RECLUSE, BUT TO LIVE ALONE
IN A CITY, IN A METROPOLIS.
THE ABOVE HOUSING NEED
IS SELDOM ADDRESSED.
THE PROPOSAL IS TO BUILD
HOUSING FOR THE SINGLE
PERSON WHO WISHES TO
LIVE IN A CITY ALONE.

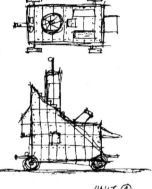

UNIT (A)

CONTINUE

(15)

SO COMPLETES THE MASQUE,
WHICH IN A WAY COMPOSED
A MASQUE IN OUR TIME.
FOR AS IT WAS NECESSARY FOR
THE HIGHLY RATIONAL-PRAGMATIC
CITY OF 15TH-CENTURY VENICE
TO CREATE MASQUES, MASKS,
MASSES FOR ITS TIME IN
ORDER TO FUNCTION, IT WOULD
APPEAR THAT WE OF OUR TIME
MUST CREATE MASQUES
(PROGRAMS ?????) FOR OUR
TIMES.

John Hejduk
august
new york 1981

4.9
John Hejduk, Berlin Masque,
1981, details.

Amid us in the world we too easily take to be real are forces that distort the authentic nature of things—blasting things into false components, holding each separate, not allowing them to touch, obstructing the smooth affiliations they should rightly maintain. The conceptual distinction between formal abstraction and figuration so popular in architectural circles in the 1970s and 1980s is one result of such distorting forces—the false notion that there can be one set of forms (grids, columns, planes, and the like) that, opaque to any meaning other than self-reflexivity, do not represent anything, and another set that refers to something outside, that is transparent to a reality but only insofar as the forms repeat what already exists. Hejduk liberates his objects from the strictures of such categorization with results that are uncanny, even monstrous.

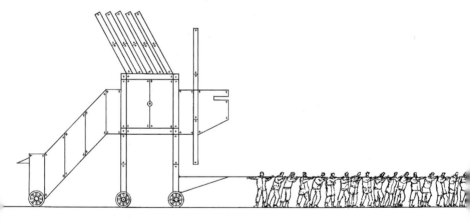

4.10
John Hejduk, Security, from the Victims series, 1986. "These elements will be moved from place to place. The townspeople of one place will move the elements to the next designated place into the hands of the receiving townspeople."

Monstrous is a word frequently heard in discussions of Hejduk's work. Here it means the refusal of the categorizations abstract or figurative, opaque or transparent, singular or typical; it means the reinscription of modernist opacity back into representation itself, but the mask also represents a situation that did not exist before its representation. If the modernist object stages the scene of the object's own production and consumption, estranging the experience and laying bare the device, then the extimate object opens to the event in which the radical unavailability of the Real is experienced. Take, for example, the Crossover Bridge of the Berlin Masque series. It is a primary figure, an archetype: a bridge (not unlike Rossi's Ponte a Bellinzona of 1974). Every formal decision can be explained in terms either of its function—a lighted passage to get across the street—or as a constructive elementalism—a geometry of tectonic components, instrumental and unambiguous in their determination. Yet it is so obviously a creature, somehow familiar but unnamable—green and spiky, unfettered by instrumental demands or formal concerns as it grazes unaware at the edge of Wilhelmstrasse. Old distinctions and categories are of no use here. Hejduk refuses the verticality of thought that separates abstraction and representation, the functional and the fantastic, buildings and animals into different registers. His chronotope is horizontal and associative, this and this and this. In it, "abstraction" (though it is wrong to continue to call it that) has a figural vocation, and function consorts with dragons.

Angels, I suppose, are monsters too of a sort. Particularly sensual angels are characteristic inhabitants of Hejduk's chronotope, positioned at the threshold of events, fumbling over their fabulously unbounded bodies to announce that something is about to happen—that a new world can be made, but not yet: we have to wait because we have not yet finished destroying the old one. We first have to chop up the old world into squares and triangles and circles and put those back together as hair and beaks and funnels and hooded eyes, because these last are more promiscuous as visual analogues, more likely to aggregate into unpredictable constellations, to sponsor unprecedented uses. And the very theatricality of these elements must be emphasized, for it is the theatrical and aleatory nature of this propped-up architecture that further bleeds off the autonomy and heroic monumentality of form. Hejduk's chronotope contains no conventional monumentality, for it lacks the stability, permanence, and memory necessary for monuments. Think again, by way of contrast, of Rossi's analogous city, sedimented out of centuries of Western culture, in which architecture is the materialization of that cultural memory. The air in Lancaster-Hanover is much thinner; the weather of Vladivostok is a vaporous, luminous, angelic time-space, the space created at the moment of the encounter, determined by architecture's gaze ("It seemed a curious mixture that simply made do with time, weather and these peoples").[25] Anachronic, anatopic, Vladivostok, Riga, Berlin, Lancaster have all undergone a kind of *dépaysement* or deterritorialization that opens up the scene for unforeseen events. Under the skies of Lake Baikal, angels rehearse the states of becoming something else while some of us on the ground perhaps worry overmuch to solve what we already are (architecture at its best has always been a practice of dissatisfaction with the way things are and has always made blueprints for something else). Hejduk's angels also nod to Mikhail Bakhtin's "grotesque body"—the body of carnival, the pre-Lenten revelry whose Dionysian potentials are most fully developed in Rabelais, according to Bakhtin, and recuperated in Bakhtin's glorification of "the material bodily lower stratum" of eating, drinking, defecation, copulation, swallowing, and regurgitation.[26] Hejduk's angelic mode, too, favors a body that transgresses its own limits, celebrating a self-unity lost to the Other. More than an attractive metaphor, the angel should therefore be understood as a primary figure in Hejduk's economy of desire. For isn't the angel—envoy of the big Other—the ultimate *objet a*?

A plaque bearing Robbe-Grillet's remark about the work of Kafka famously hung in John Hejduk's office: "The hallucinatory effect derives from the extraordinary clarity and not from mystery or mist. Nothing is more fantastic ultimately than precision."[27] Part of one's attraction to, but also dismay in the face of, the characters of the masques is the incommensurable distance between the precision and fineness of the drawings—the clarity and efficiency with which they describe the geometry and tectonics of objects are so controlled as to be almost cold, engineered, mechanical—and the depth and complexity of emotion they conjure. All of the literature on Hejduk's work points in some way to this latter effect. Some writers claim to be able to channel through his objects the most horrifying of modernity's forces (the project Victims [1986] comprising 67 entities surely refers to a concentration camp). Others find joyous, almost comic enclosures to protect them or distract them from the same. Surely, somehow, both are right. For what these otherwise opposing perceptions share is an existential uncertainty generated by the affective precision of the architecture itself: the recognition of the fact that our cultural identities, our very foundations, are outside ourselves, in the clusters of images and codes through which we are culturally apprehended. As with Lacan's gaze, which he once termed "the presence of others as such," so with Hejduk's masques: in both we confront the fact that our subjectivity depends on the symbolic ratification of the Other and how we take our place in that encounter.

When we recognize that we exist as subjects only by and for some Other with whom we can have no audience, we may react with fear, even guilt, but also, perhaps, with renewed ambition and determination. Interestingly, Jean-Paul Sartre's *Being and Nothingness* of 1943, from which Lacan draws his own meditations on the gaze, characterizes this decentering of the self in terms of an insistently Christian thematics: our self-definition, our dependency on the Other, is a lapse into a "fallen" state that is registered as a visual exchange between subject and object; a certain failure is a requisite of redemption.[28] More than any other contemporary architect, Hejduk broods on our fall from grace, on constitutive absence and the necessity of loss, on our possible redemption, and how these can be figured in the moment of architecture. The architecture of Christ's cross becomes Hejduk's figure for such themes. "What always interests me in the old paintings of the crucifixion is the construction of the cross. How the cross was constructed. How it was detailed. I think it is important to know."[29] But, of course, it's not about construction alone. Hejduk is aware that the cross was interpreted by Mondrian in a mystical sense, while Le Corbusier and Loos saw in it an erotics at the level of the mark. As well as being spatially and tectonically precise, the simplest and most elementary mark, the cross is the focus of the themes of individuality and collectivity, unspeakable loss and humbling plenitude, which Hejduk returns to again and again in his later work. The cross is the mark of the felt loss of architecture's original, divine mission of founding a promised land—a church on solid ground—and the necessary covering over of the site of that loss, masking it with architecture itself.[30] The cross is the architectural Thing that materializes unfathomable mysteries (virgin birth, incarnation, resurrection) and unattainable cultural enjoyments, the kernel around which the subject can only circle. Somewhere among these attributes are suggestions that may explain why Hejduk, in his last works, turned to an overtly religious imagery, but without ever swerving from his experimentation with architecture's most basic elements and deepest structures. Perhaps it is the cross rather than the square or the diamond that is architecture's most primitive form. It is, no doubt, the most profound architectural element in Hejduk's terms of a double articulation of formal and tectonic development together with viewer-subject construction—the degree zero of the architectural sign. And it is under the sign of the cross that Hejduk brings his image-screen, his elevational chronotope, to its final form.

Hejduk's conviction that architecture produces encounters with collective cultural memories, that it deals fundamentally with the fragility of physical and spiritual sanctuary, and that the subject and object of architecture are engaged in reciprocal address and constitution—all these themes are brought to an awesome intensity in his last works. His first steps toward that are radically architectural, layering form upon form and manipulating them to a maximum. Cathedral is the most complex single object of his career, gathering up the most significant of his prior formal inventions and repeating and collapsing them onto a simple rectangular volume. Or perhaps it is a thick wall, with all the being-together of diverse elements on the vertical plane that his Wall apparatus captures. The original Berlin Masque building (which itself cannibalizes the Retreat Masque and Wall House 3) operates as Cathedral's armature. Various other characters from the Berlin Masque are there; Wall House 3 reappears, now as one element of another wall; several small chapels and single-volume units accrue to the elevations; the Collapse of Time tower is on the roof; and the various Morandi-like light canons, funnels, and tubes that he experimented with in his architectural still lifes return. Cathedral seems to have been intended as a summation; and in this regard it is telling that just after the Canadian Centre for Architecture completed the model of Cathedral, Hejduk began working on A Gathering, his unfinished site plan for a giant masque (or perhaps the masque has become the entire town) that was to contain the footprint of every project he ever made. It is as if in these works he is cataloging all the ways he had tried momentarily to arrest the unlocalizable architectural gaze.

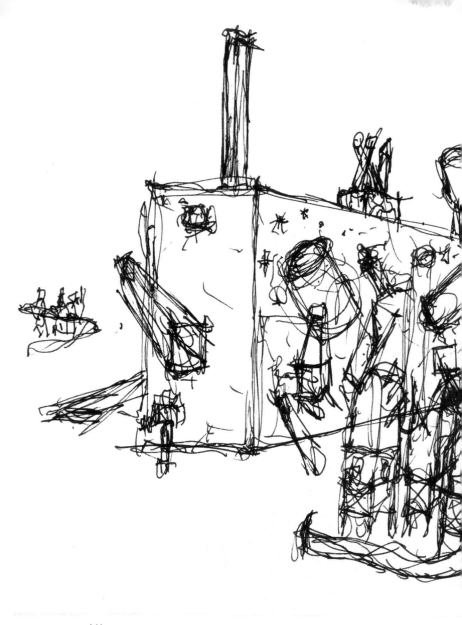

4.11
John Hejduk, Cathedral, 1996, sketch.
Canadian Centre for Architecture.

But given Hejduk's penchant for binary conceptual organizations, is it not also significant that he was working at the same time on the series of thirty-two Enclosures?[31] We know from correspondence that he considered Enclosures to be among the most important of his last works. Are they related in some way to Cathedral? Synthesizing the apocalyptic scenes of the tenth-century Morgan Beatus, Giotto's *Saint Francis* cycle, and, at the other end of art historical time, Barnett Newman's zip paintings; exploring penetrations through walls and occupations of single-room sanctuaries; creating landscapes interfused and haunted by objects, Enclosures compresses some of Hejduk's favorite themes into astonishingly simple gestures. If Cathedral is architecture's maximization, Enclosures is the absolute reduction and essentialization beyond which his architecture could not go. Accumulation is one way of making manifest the structures and codes that underlie perception, an end-of-the-line strategy in which an array of variations on a theme make the theme more precise. The reuse, again and again, of Wall House 3—in Cemetery for the Ashes of Thought, in Berlin Masque, and its final return in Cathedral—is an example of this sort of pondering. But after the early Diamond Houses and Wall Houses, Hejduk tried to reach through this sort of complexity of accrual—the complexity that results from the piling up of form in Cathedral or A Gathering—to a place beyond the end of the line, where one might glimpse the foundations of formalization itself. And for that, synthesis and reduction are necessary—the kind of peeling away of form evident in Enclosures that seeks the matrix beneath. The Enclosures can be placed in Hejduk's schema, chronologically and logically, as the second term of a binary that begins with the Cathedral, as the dialectical opposition along the same axis of summation and closure, the necessary complementary device for his post-endgame signification.

How are we to read the Enclosures? In a set of drawings called Sanctuary, now held in the Menil Collection, and another set for a project entitled Chapel, Wedding of the Moon and the Sun, given by Hejduk to Charles Gwathmey, all made after Cathedral and Christ Chapel and probably just before Enclosures, there are several sketches of sanctuaries and chapels, triangular in plan, with crucifixes suspended at various angles. "I desired the most simple structure for the space and its relationship," writes Hejduk in his explanation of Chapel. And indeed it is as if his early diagram of the origin of the space of the present (the transformation of the diamond into a vertical plane shown in figure 4.1) has now found a final variant of its form, neither diamond nor wall but the stage in between—a diamond in the process of flattening, a diamond-becoming-wall. As did the diamond in plan and the wall in elevation, now the simple triangular space functions volumetrically to produce the dialectical relationship between depth and flatness. But the diagrams of this space resemble nothing so much as Lacan's diagram of the gaze, of vision turned back on itself. And the cross suspended in the triangular chapel and backlit by sunlight focused through a sunburst-shaped window, notwithstanding its clear and undeniable Christian meanings, functions primarily as a Wall-like apparatus, Lacan's *dompte-regard*—an image-screen or mask that both focuses and tames the architectural gaze and mediates the sheer power of cumulative spatial experience into a form both semblable and strange. For this is not an ordinary Christian icon; something is being done to the crucifix, and it is being done *architecturally* (just as in the Diamond Houses, the Wall Houses, and the Collapse of Time), by tilting planes through space, by setting up impossible orders (astronomic alignments, for example), by conflating incommensurable worlds, all of which challenge our optical-geometrical mastery of space and install *us*, as well, in the larger picture. Hejduk's crucifix is analogous to devices other artists have used when a powerful

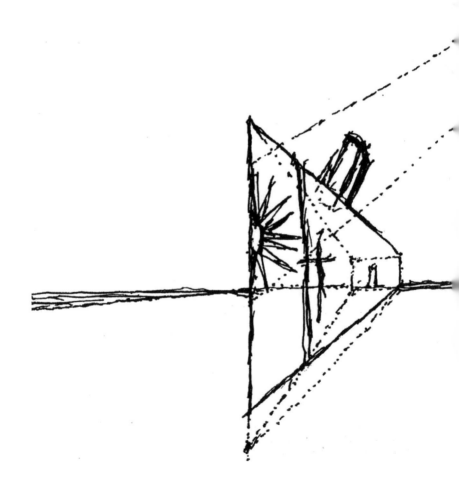

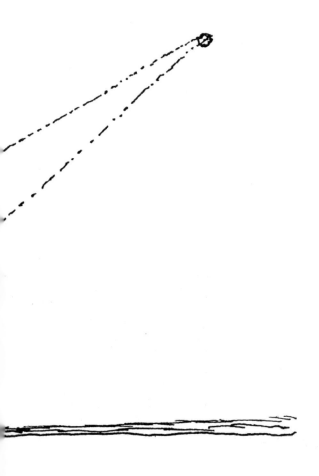

4.12
[two parts] John Hejduk, Chapel, Wedding
of the Moon and Sun, 1998, sketch.
Collection of Charles Gwathmey.

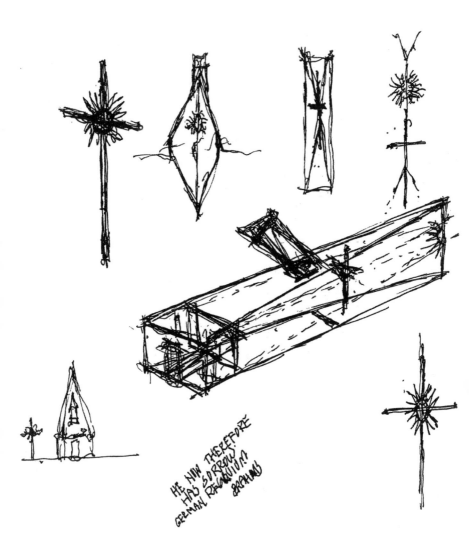

HE NOW THEREFORE
HAS SORROW
GERMAN REQUIEM
BRAHMS

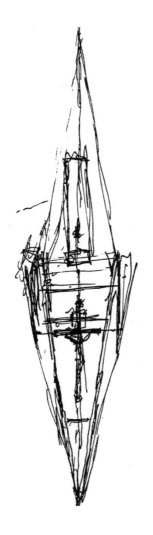

technique had to be brought to some sort of closure, to an absolute inwardness or, equally, to an absolute exteriority—extimacy. Consider, for example, the *Last Supper* of Leonardo, where the vanishing point of the Renaissance's perspective system pierces the halo of Christ; or the way Malevich hung his *Black Square* like an icon across the corner of the gallery in the "0,10" exhibition; or Le Corbusier's *Open Hand*; or Robert Wilson's *14 Stations*; or *The Stations of the Cross* by Newman, whom Hejduk particularly admired. The point is that religious imagery has historically provided art with the most widely understandable code for its attempts at transcending this unsatisfactory world or proposing some other to put in its place. By the time of Enclosures, Hejduk's architecture had outgrown the formal system he had spent his life developing. He had to find a new device of signification to progress beyond it. Or, perhaps, a very old one.

There is one reading of Enclosures, then, that is too literal but nonetheless correct: that they are analogues and elaborations of Hejduk's cross. The Enclosures are scenes that one might view as murals in Hejduk's various chapels; they are the stained-glass windows of the sanctuaries, the luminous membranes that separate worlds with manageable encodings of the Thing we cannot bear to behold. The Enclosures are the Wall, whose anthropomorphic building parts hovering in air have now become human: the spiky hair of the Berlin Masque creatures is now a crown of thorns, the V-shaped roofs have become angel wings, the horned creatures of Museum of War and Peace have evolved into bulls; the triangular plan is tilted up vertically like a cubist's table. The actors are sandwiched and separated by thin registers, allowing angels and bulls, martyrs and mourners to slide past one another, while the architecture minimally frames their movements— invoking its pre-perspectival, narrative vocation in medieval painting, to provide the setting in which the action can be played out. Enclosures is Hejduk's answer to Giotto's *Saint Francis* series, with its floating Christ, holy rays, and spewing stigmata. And to Le Corbusier, who wrote, "I have not experienced the miracle of faith but I have often known the miracle of inexpressible space."[32]

More precisely, the Enclosures are the traits of Architecture's gaze first sought for in the Diamond Houses and Wall Houses: the nearly theological revelation of architecture's history (pre-perspectival space through cubist space, up to the present), the inscription of otherness in the field of vision, the face that looks back at us, the mask and the masque that subdue and negotiate meanings and experiences too awesome for us to see directly. "The face crystallizes all redundancies, it emits and receives, releases and recaptures signifying signs. It is a whole body unto itself: it is like the body of the center of signifiance [the process of signification] to which all of the deterritorialized signs affix themselves, and it marks the limit of their deterritorialization. . . . The face is what gives the signifier substance. . . . The mask does not hide the face, it *is* the face."[33] This passage is from Deleuze and Guattari's chapter on "faciality," the name given to the condition or production of a specific, though provisional, authorization and regulation of visual images out of a proliferation of signification and subjectification. And it could also describe Hejduk's last works. Like the Wall, the face is conceived as a signifying surface: "Signifiance is never without a white wall upon which it inscribes its signs and redundancies."[34] Faciality restricts the polyvocality of signs and the constructedness of subjects even as it draws on and retains some of their excessive potential. In Hejduk's case, the "faciality" of Enclosures was necessary to oppose and contain the limitless signification of Cathedral, necessary to overcome the entropy inherent in such an endlessly circulating formal system as his.

4.13
John Hejduk, bird's-eye view of
structures overlooking Cathedral
site, 1996.

In his last works, Hejduk found himself facing contradictions between a dream of fullness of experience and profundity of meaning, on the one hand, and a vision of the real limits of what architecture can do, the lack built into its representational system. The Enclosures mark the limit condition of architectural signification and coordinate an entire regime of loss and desired redemption, which the Christian imagery helps to represent. Deleuze and Guattari also put the face of Christ in the center of faciality's regime. Christ is the Western cultural gaze, the writer of codes, the standard against which variation and deviation are measured—my semblable and my stranger. And facialization is effected, at least in part, by stigmata, the trace of a limit condition. Faciality is the visible mark of pathos but also the promise of getting beyond it (didn't the resurrected, transformed Christ admonish Thomas to probe the wound that had guaranteed mankind's salvation?). The Enclosures are the architectural stigmata on the corpus of Hejduk's work. They trace a certain failure or loss—the moment in which architecture glimpses its inadequacy—but they hold out the possibility of new orders and perceptions. "Now is the time for drawing angels," Hejduk insisted, the time for keeping that possibility always in sight.

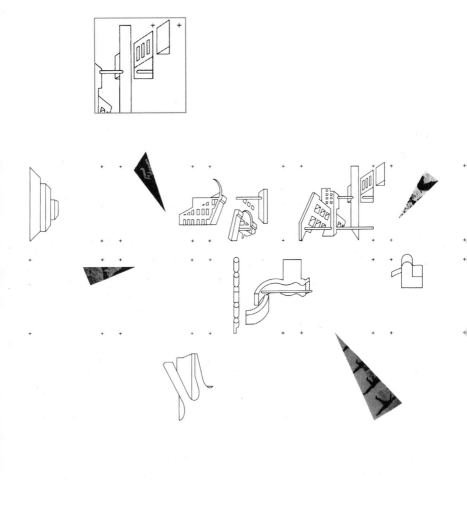

SPACING

But an overemphasis on architecture's wounds obscures the jouissance with which the stigmata are received. Aware of the fundamental lack at the center of architecture, Bernard Tschumi pursued "the pleasure of architecture" (which was the title of an early essay and could be the label for his *oeuvre complète*), tracking an architectural experience of a different kind than we have seen thus far. Like others of the late avant-garde, though, he probed architecture at its ontological boundary. And there, at the limits of the architectural Symbolic, the Real makes itself felt not in the substance but rather in the failures and duplicities of the architectural signifier. As Tschumi put it, "Behind all masks lie 'dark' and unconscious streams that cannot be dissociated from the pleasure of architecture. The mask may exalt appearances. Yet by its very presence, it says that, in the background, there is 'something else.'"[1] Tschumi, perhaps more fully than any other of the late avant-garde, recognized that the "something else"—the architectural Real—is both the hard, impenetrable core that resists discursive appropriation (it is prior to symbolization) and at the same time the exorbitant emptiness that remains after symbolization is complete (even as it is produced by symbolization itself). Its issue, therefore, is both trauma and jouissance (a suffering enjoyed). And it can never be translated or rendered knowable as a positivity, this architectural Real, but only experienced through an unassimilable, negative Other—spaced out and projected backward, as it were, out of its own structural effects.

In a set of essays written in 1975–1976, Tschumi takes account of the state of architectural discourse at that time and stakes out a territory in the field that he believes he can productively occupy.[2] In particular, the essays are a meditation on the opposition between architecture as a product of the mind—a conceptual and dematerialized discipline with its own consistent logic—and architecture as the sensual experience and practice of space— a spatial *punctum* that resists and exceeds study and analysis, whose status is fundamentally corporeal and contingent. In the earliest of the essays, "Questions of Space: The Pyramid and the Labyrinth (or the Architectural Paradox)," Tschumi formulates the self-designation and reflexivity of architecture's autonomy thesis first in Hegelian terms: as an image of *Geist*'s progressive attempts to overcome matter, architecture is by its nature involved with building but not reducible to building (think of the ancient pyramids as proclaiming or symbolizing the presence of an inner entity, a spirit and concept, to which their built form is manifestly extrinsic). Architecture is an "artistic supplement," a set of concepts added to the image and experience of a building. Or conversely, as Tschumi puts it, the "functional and technical characteristics of a house or a temple [are] the means to an end that excluded those very characteristics."[3]

By 1975 we could recognize that architecture is, above all, the production of experiences and concepts and not necessarily just of built objects. But Tschumi also insisted on the paradox that if architecture is a specific kind of imagination (an intimate blend of sensing, imaging, and conceptualization), which schematizes the world in irreducibly architectural ways, it is also a particular kind of Imaginary, which produces a particular kind of desire (that is, Architecture), which finds its way to the surface of representation in a surprising variety of practices and expressions. Architecture, then, has everything to do with a particular impulse finding its representation—and thereby its sensual expression and libidinal investment—in different media, and is only contingently related to the composition of a building. Hence the paradox of the time: that through imaging and conceptualization "the architect could finally achieve the sensual satisfaction that the making of material objects no longer provided."[4] Tschumi was thinking about Hegel, Kant, Lacan, and Barthes at a time when the ruling doctrine of functionalism was being dismantled; but he is thinking *like* the Adorno of the essay "Functionalism Today": "Space and the sense of space can become more than impoverished purpose only when imagination impregnates them with purposefulness. *Imagination breaks out of the immanent connections of purpose, to which it owes its very existence*."[5] It is the last sentence, of course, where the dialectic bursts open a conception of architecture as more than either function or thing, that resonates with Tschumi's formulation of function and technique as "the means to an end that excluded those very characteristics."

While such a postfunctionalist, pro-conceptual declamation captures the prevalent mood of progressive architecture in the mid-1970s, Tschumi moves through his analysis to a more distinctive conclusion. First, he poses the ideological dilemma of the autonomy project, which he seems almost alone in recognizing, namely, "If the architectural piece renounces its autonomy by recognizing its latent ideological and financial dependency, it accepts the mechanisms of society. If it sanctuarizes itself, in an art-for-art's-sake position, it does not escape classification among existing ideological compartments."[6] A nondialectical autonomy thesis would only assure the entropy of desire and the disinvestment of the libidinal object. Even the utopian energies of the radical architectures of the 1960s, especially Archizoom and Superstudio, with whom Tschumi clearly sympathizes, eventually devolved into a "desperate attempt" to de-conceal the materials and forces of ideology, "ironically verifying where the system was going," and thus becoming (merely) ideological themselves.

By the time of Tschumi's writing, "architecture seemed to have gained autonomy by opposing the institutional framework. But in the process it had become the institutional opposition, thus growing into everything it tried to oppose."[7]

Tschumi meets this ideological dilemma with an Adorno-like strategy of negation: "So architecture seems to survive only whenever it negates itself, whenever it saves its nature by negating the form that society expects of it. *I would therefore suggest that there has never been any reason to doubt the necessity of architecture, for the necessity of architecture is its non-necessity. It is useless but radically so.* Its radicalism constitutes its very strength in a society where profit is prevalent." He then nods to Adorno directly. "Rather than an obscure artistic supplement or a cultural justification for financial manipulations, architecture is not unlike fireworks, for these 'empirical apparitions,' as Adorno puts it, 'produce a delight that cannot be sold or bought, that has no exchange value and cannot be integrated in the production cycle.'"[8] Tschumi here deconstructs Tafuri's assessment of contemporary architecture's "sublime uselessness" by radicalizing uselessness itself, giving uselessness a creative social force. There is no avant-garde that is not only enabled but also contained by what it opposes. Even transgression must be sanctioned as such in order to be effective. Long past is the possibility of prescribing a renewed normality for architecture in terms of function, performance, cultural representation, or social service. Rather, we must now see the conflicts and discontents of a discipline and a practice that, in order to have a vocation at all in the cultural world, must refuse unflinchingly to conform to cultural expectations: architecture's unhappy consciousness. Tschumi announces his conclusion with all the force of Hegelian inevitability:

This means, in effect, that, perhaps for the first time in history, architecture can never be. The effect of the great battles of social programs is obliterated, and so is the security of archetypes. Defined by its questioning, architecture is the expression of a lack, a shortcoming, a noncompletion [Lacan's manqué à être]. It always misses something, either reality or concept. Architecture is both being and non-being. The only alternative to the paradox is silence, a final nihilistic statement that might provide modern architectural history with its ultimate punchline, its self-annihilation.[9]

Architecture's *Sein zum Tode*. But we already know of desire's fundamental relation to death: when architecture follows its desire to the limit condition, what opens up is a radical nonbeing that nevertheless is not a mere nothing.

That architecture, since it clearly had a beginning, might also have an end is easy enough to conceptualize in the Hegelian scheme of things. That one might actively seek its end was made all the more plausible when, in the 1960s, we began to focus on the profound complicity of cultural institutions and university systems, not to mention the construction and development industries, with state power and the perpetuation of the status quo. But Tschumi's meditations on the Hegelian supplement and the death of architecture, it seems to me, are less motivated by the end-of-art debates, already well rehearsed if not over by 1975, than by a different dawning awareness of the particular historical fatedness of architecture itself—of a specific cultural production, perhaps the most deeply social of all, now inevitably suffering its own unique, historically determined recontainment, reterritorialization, and implosion after more than two centuries of opening, transgression, and revolt. By 1975—in the face of devastating economic recession, the first energy crisis, as well as the weariness of the Vietnam war—architecture's imminent end had become less a matter of willful self-annihilation than the far less spectacular fading away of its social relevance compared to other cultural practices (like film, video, graphic design, and visual culture generally).

And yet, though architecture is necessarily transmitted by a sanctioned set of texts and institutional practices, there is the "something else" that remains forever intractable to that discursive corpus. While the discourse of autonomy in its weaker forms reduces architecture to the mere availability of preexisting elements and combinatory techniques from some positive stock, which can be used to produce or reproduce meaning, Tschumi recognizes that architectural autonomy itself must be volatilized, that the internal and intimate must be exteriorized. How, in other words, could architecture face its death in a way adequate to its desire? Rossi's transcendental, presuppositional structure of the City already tried to account for the singularity of the architectural imagination. What Tschumi's work will insist on is that that structure, architecture's big Other, by its very actuality in architectural discourse is also always already defective, insufficient—"the expression of a lack, a shortcoming, a noncompletion." There is never enough meaning to close the gap opened by the Other. And it is precisely this insufficiency and uselessness of signification that corresponds to architectural jouissance—a particular self-enclosed, autotelic moment in architecture that is simultaneously architecture's own undoing. "Jouissance is forbidden to he who speaks," instructed Lacan.[10] Such a dimension can have no identifiable object as its referent; it cannot be included in the economy of communication; it is not "about something"—it can be understood only through the effort *to bring about*.

To this end, in the last sections of "The Architectural Paradox" Tschumi offers a brief, tentative mention of a possible alternative to architecture's self-annihilation and silence, one that might accelerate and intensify the architectural paradox rather than mollify it: he calls it "experienced space," which, more than a perception or a concept of space, is a process, a way of practicing space irreducible to the generalizing equivalence of meaning making—an event. For Tschumi, *event* was a highly charged term: it represented a reversal of the object-subject hierarchy of contemporaneous architecture, and it was related both to the situationists' *événement* ("whose symbolic and exemplary value lay in their seizure of urban space and not in the design of what was built") and to Georges Bataille's *expérience intérieure* (the pyramid and labyrinth of Tschumi's title are from Bataille's *Eroticism*)—two of Tschumi's emotional and intellectual role models, who were largely unconsidered by architects at the time. Like Hejduk's encounter with the architectural gaze, which also signals a moment of perception, *event* for Tschumi involves a material registration and condensation of the role of cultural, historical, and economic determinants in architectural experience—a radical singularity of happening. Different from Hejduk, however, and importantly so, event now figures as an effect of architectural program and performance together with form, rather than of form alone. Tschumi later illustrates the notion of an event with examples of "cross-programming" like pole vaulting in a cathedral (the cathedral's sectional disposition being exquisitely conducive to such misuse), bicycling in the laundromat (a Vertov-like montage of intermoving circles), sky diving in the elevator shaft. "Murder [function] in the Street [form] differs from Murder [same function] in the Cathedral [different form] . . . Radically." Tschumi's architecture of events appears dialectically as a possible third term between the contradiction of autonomy and negation; not a dialectical resolution, it is, rather,

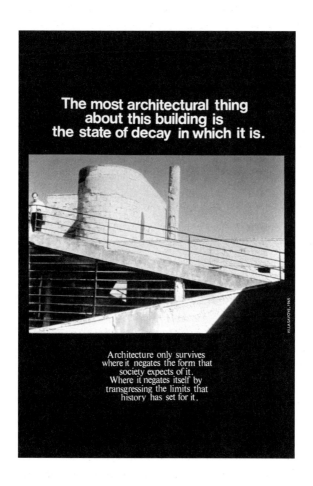

The most architectural thing
about this building is
the state of decay in which it is.

Architecture only survives
where it negates the form that
society expects of it.
Where it negates itself by
transgressing the limits that
history has set for it.

5.1
Bernard Tschumi, Advertisements
for Architecture (1 of 9 parts),
c. 1975.

a spacing out of architecture's autonomy and its negation to make a place for the architectural event. Indeed, it should reveal the productivity of that contradiction even as it dissolves it into a space of improvisation, variation, ramification, and difference. It is this revelation (perhaps not too strong a word) that is announced in the early essays and that Tschumi's subsequent work enacts.

At the same time Tschumi was writing "The Architectural Paradox," he was also working on Advertisements for Architecture, a series of postcard-sized montages of image and text that included references to Bataille, Jorge Luis Borges, Tennessee Williams, T. S. Eliot, a B-movie adaptation of a Raymond Chandler story, pleasure gardens, and bondage scenes. Two of the Advertisements featured photographs Tschumi had taken of the Villa Savoye in 1965, while he was a student at the ETH in Zurich, where he found "the squalid walls of the small service rooms on the ground floor, stinking of urine, smeared with excrement, and covered with obscene graffiti."[11] How should we read these Advertisements? When they have been read at all, they have been seen as an explicit alternative to the overprivileging of pure, autonomous form by Aldo Rossi, Peter Eisenman, and others (known in the 1970s as the "Whites") and to Colin Rowe's influential preference for the uncorrupted, pristine *physique*-flesh of Le Corbusier. Surely this reading is correct as far as it goes: Tschumi's "Architecture and Transgression," the text that accompanied the publication of parts of the Advertisements in *Oppositions* 7 in 1976, returns to the themes of "The Architectural Paradox" and reintroduces the transgressive eroticism of Bataille explicitly against his contemporary Le Corbusier. "The contradiction between architectural concept and sensual experience of space resolves itself at one point of tangency: *the rotten point* ['where glass meets mold,' as one of the Advertisements has it], the very point that taboos and culture have always rejected."[12]

But Tschumi augments this elsewhere, describing the Advertisements project in a slightly different way as a notational device to "trigger" the desire for architecture—not an architecture of objects but rather (acknowledging the central lack involved) of a "point of tangency": the embodied jouissance beyond form's legibility, opened up in the lack of its own signifying finality. Stressing the inevitable commodification of architecture's image, he queries the possibility of détourning and accelerating rather than resisting that inevitability into an erotics of architectural performance. Tschumi writes, "The usual function of advertisements . . . is to trigger desire for something beyond the [image or form] itself. . . . As there are advertisements for products, why not advertisements for architecture?"[13] This is advertising in libidinal terms—intensities, perversions, transgression, and violence—following Bataille, no doubt, but also the cultural politics of *Tel Quel*: making art from the world "just as it is," only more so; pushing art through the channels of commodity distribution and perception in order to dialectically produce a new kind of perception and, at the limit of the push, let art annihilate itself (once again confirming the bonds between desire, transgression, and death).[14]

By replacing conventional architectural drawings with other notational systems (here photographs and texts) that trigger or open a space for a possible architectural experience, Advertisements for Architecture throws into difficulty the sorting through of the relays between author, object, performance, audience, and so forth. For example, is the author here Tschumi, Le Corbusier, or those who smeared the excrement? Is the architectural content already present before the photograph that reduplicates it, or is content there only in the combination of photograph and text? Or is there no content at all, but only an organization of various flows of desire produced by a specific reader and then only in a particular moment? Tschumi attempts to establish architectural notation as a process of telegraphic overproduction that is not secondary to some building it denotes (as are conventional architectural drawings) and has no predetermined relationship to the architectural performance it solicits or triggers. The notational system simply frames a space for and sets in motion a generalized architectural potential, an enabling condition comprising a derivation (Le Corbusier's villa) and distortion (the photograph of its squalid condition), an augmentation (the captions), and, importantly, a gap—a desire that must be performed by each reader of these works. "It is not the clash between fragments of architecture that counts," instructs one of the Advertisements, "but the invisible movement between them. Desire." Not architecture itself is offered but only evidence that it exists: a proclamation of existence made by refusing presence and evoking "something else."

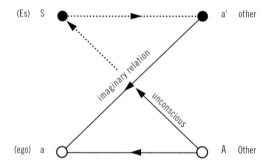

5.2
Jacques Lacan, L Schema.
From *Écrits*.

The peculiar visual machinery of Advertisements corresponds to that archaic stage of subject production Lacan termed the Imaginary. The subject of desire here is nothing less than architecture itself—architecture as such, but beyond the limit where, as substance, it has already been lost. Lacan's so-called L Schema from *Écrits* famously constructs the subject of desire as an effect of a dynamic structure of internal contradictions—including a relationship between the subject (S on the top left in the graph), the desired object (a´, on the top right, the *objet petite autre*, denizen of the Imaginary), and that object's double, the ego (a under S), which in this case can be understood to designate the Advertisements' mimicry of the commercialized, eroticized milieu in which they have appeared. The system of desire (indicated by a´) is opposed to the system of identifications (indicated by a). The shifting, reflecting, doubled relationship between the object and the object-effect that is the ego is indicated in the graph by the diagonal line, which must be read both as a vector of desire flowing between a and a´ and also as having an implicit planar dimension, which is to say that it is also the image-screen of Lacan's mirror stage, as is made explicit by the label "imaginary relation," the interaction staged by the mirror. Written into this schema, Advertisements provides the objects of desire primarily as texts and images, of course, immanent to the works themselves—the "morselized" photographs of the Villa Savoye are nothing if not *objets a*, but so are the ropes and fatal falls and movie references (Tschumi is an absolute master at constructing appropriated images as intense but forever-lost objects of desire). But the objects themselves are nothing without the flow of desire, which they produce but which also acts as their support. The setting up of the *objets a* as triggers, the presentation of them as substitutes for an architecture we desire but do not have, construes them as signifiers and mirrors them back to the viewer as marks of a specific, even unique and personal, affective architectural encounter—an event: *this* moment of experience, *this* sensation of architecture condensed *here*, *this* spacing for architecture that happened for *me* just *now*. *C'est donc moi, c'est donc à moi.*[15] Such is the performative dimension of this work—to constitute the desire for architecture out of an impossible-to-fill lack, figured by part-objects in a flash of recognition.

All this so far has taken place on the side of the Imaginary, where the architectural subject is elicited by a movement of desire through part-objects in an act of enunciation, an experience, a performance. But as the L Schema makes clear, the more fundamental relationship that mediates all of this machinery is that between S, the subject of desire, and a big Other, A. Reading Advertisements through the complete L Schema forces the recognition that the flows of desire structuring the viewer's experience are projected from and return to the locus of that Other, which Lacan calls the Symbolic (or language, or law, or the unconscious itself, defined as the "discourse of the Other"). Architecture, the subject of desire, is not produced willfully in an intentional act; rather, it is the effect of what is repressed. Note that in the graph, the image-screen absorbs the vector of the unconscious and blocks its representation, even as desire is an effect of the unconscious. At the time of Advertisements, Tschumi does not give a name to A, the Other of this Symbolic realm. But we know it already: it is City.

Recall the main argument of the autonomy thesis: that the production of architecture results from a practice of a very specific and precise kind, whose enabling conditions antedate any particular architectural project. The designer does not fabricate the materials he works with: the materials of architecture—its elements and operations, its types and procedures—are not neutral and open to a unification imposed by the architect. Rather, the materials of architecture possess a specific character and formative potential of their own that, while creating conditions for elaboration and expansion, more emphatically impose constraint, demand conservation, and compel constant repetition. Architectural decisions are already determined by the discourse itself: the architect neither invents nor chooses them. The architect discovers rather than creates the project, encounters situations rather than devises solutions. Therefore, in a certain sense, if the architectural system is autonomous, there is nothing that can be added to it, notwithstanding the illusion of choice, and there is nothing to do with it except to continue it in the hope that mere continuance will increase experience and understanding. This system is what we have called the City.

Thus the City is a determinant of architecture; or, put another way, architecture as the subject of desire is a City effect. At the same time, however, there is the haunting resonance that the whole thing could have been set up differently, that the entire architectural Symbolic and its authority are a fragile artifice. But rather than free the practice of architecture from its autonomy, this arbitrariness further enforces the constraints of autonomy through the recognition that its necessity is not derived from the Real but rather an elaborate fiction added to it, a negation that gives rise to a chain of metonymic associations, libidinal substitutions, and empty intervals. According to this account the very making of architecture is a spacing out of the architectural Symbolic that cannot be concluded or sublated, only rehearsed—endlessly unto death. Architecture must constantly be reiterated, repeated *as architecture*, constructed as subject of desire, which, on a trajectory through the architectural Imaginary, returns to the symbolic City, which is also architecture's record, the storehouse where the endless reiterations are inventoried. Then through a kind of *Nachträglichkeit*, that repetition is crossed in the opposite direction by the vector of the architectural unconscious, the discourse of the Other. Thus is the City the beginning and end of both trajectories.

By defining architecture as, on the one hand, a repetition born of very precise beginnings and enabling conditions and, on the other, a performance and production of unprecedented desires and experiences, Tschumi initiated a crisis in these early works but also a potential in architecture that has been barely acknowledged, even as subsequent developments up to our own time seem to develop his predictions. Indeed, his particular differentiation of architecture from its medium, made in these early essays and conceptual projects, will later be developed to eventually mark the extreme limits of the Hegelian supplement, that is, of autonomy as such, turning architecture's autonomy into what we now perceive, according to contemporary theoretical discourse, as its very opposite—the pure production of effects. But in Tschumi's work, beginning as early as 1975, it is as if through a spacing and exteriorization of architecture's autonomy we have already tunneled through to the other side, to the side of effects (like the electron in quantum theory that is on both sides of a barrier at the same time), finding within the autonomy project a practice that tries to keep faith with some more fundamental state of contingency, delirium, and euphoria of repetition rather than either an affirmation of form or a melancholy of loss. In 1975–1976 Tschumi announced what would become the legacy of the most advanced avant-garde practice: architecture can maintain itself *in effect* even as the moment to realize it in actuality has passed.

The Manhattan Transcripts (1976–1981) push this research explicitly toward the urban scale, for it is now Manhattan, rather than the Villa Savoye, that is the cathexis object—a city ready for *détournement*, understood as having an erotic, transgressive, and violent programmatic potential woven into its grid of streets and avenues.

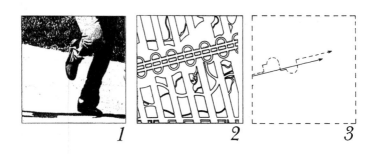

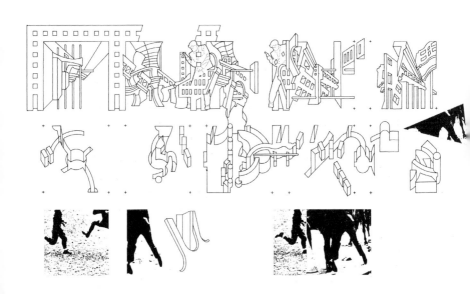

5.3
Bernard Tschumi, Manhattan Transcripts,
1976–1981, selections.

> *Programmatic violence ought to be there* a contrario, *to*
> *question past humanist programs that strictly cover only*
> *functional requirements necessary for survival and pro-*
> *duction, and to favor those activities generally considered*
> *negative and unproductive: "luxury, mourning, wars,*
> *cults; the construction of sumptuous monuments, games,*
> *spectacles, arts; perverse sexual activity." The concept of*
> *violence also suggests different readings of spatial func-*
> *tion—in the intersection of logic and pain, rationality*
> *and anguish, concept and pleasure.*[16]

The internal quotation is from Bataille's "The Notion of Expenditure," and Tschumi is meditating particularly on Bataille's
notion of "nonproductive expenditure," with its emphasis on
loss, destruction, and transgression as modes of jouissance.[17]
Nonproductive expenditure values process and means over objects
and ends; it recognizes that the possibility of excess without limits is bound up with violence. The point of Tschumi's repeated
references to violence in Advertisements and the Manhattan
Transcripts should not be misunderstood as simply a rebellious
toying with the taboo. Rather, what is at stake for Tschumi is the
generation of domains of untranslatable multiplicity and difference, domains and forces that disrupt and violate one another
because of their nonidentity.[18]

The Transcripts are presented in tripartite diagrams: the photographic fragments (events) now act as a code for the architectural
program—a murder in Central Park and the flight of the fugitive
to the simulated pleasures of pornography and prostitution on
Forty-second Street. The architectural drawings (spaces) are
distortions of traditional cities and gardens (drawn in a manner
that obliquely refers to the constructivist projects of Iakov Chernikov
and Natan Altman). And the fugitive's flight is traced in a choreo-
graphic notation of lines and arrows (movements) tracing flows

and interactions. These three notational bands produce aleatoric drifts and interactions both horizontally and vertically in the same way the street grid and buildings of Manhattan do, but in perhaps an even more multidimensional and heterogeneous space of constructed and appropriated significations. The Manhattan Transcripts can be understood as a refolding of Guy Debord's *Naked City* map of 1957, with its temporalization of space and its passional and violent drifts through metropolitan terrains. *The Naked City* was itself an appropriation of a 1948 film noir about a murder in Manhattan, and the film was in turn an appropriation of a book of crime photographs by Weegee (a.k.a. Arthur Fellig). But Tschumi recodes and rescripts these references and others into a systematic mapping of event space.[19]

It is instructive to consider Tschumi's own recollection of the project:

> *Traditional means of representation—perspectives, axonometrics, plans, sections—have a number of limitations. The idea of the event, for instance, which had evolved out of my previous theoretical work, could not be represented through these means. But it had been extensively documented in other disciplines such as dance, certain sports, and film theory, as well as in the work of a number of performance artists. The diagrams I then elaborated were crucial in order to bring a sort of spatial abstraction, much as in the work of a mathematician who operates through formulas and equations. In an analogous way I decided to use the equivalent of equations—in this case, architectural notation. I had always been interested in the fact that architecture was not only about space but also about the movement of bodies in that space. What fascinated me at the time of the* Transcripts, *and still does, is that I could take a program and dismantle it, cut*

it up, and reconfigure it in the same way as I could with
any visual material. In fact, the location of the pieces of
the program is architecture. In other words, this was not
unlike writing a script for a film: one could have a murder
at the beginning and a murder at the end, or two murders
in the middle. [20]

The actors (and we the readers) do not move in space so much as space moves with them (and us) as a constantly permutating *Umwelt* delineated as distorted architectural fragments, unfolding in perspective, transforming across time. In many of the frames, the horizon is withheld, the vanishing point of the perspective unnaturally high or low, the shapes morphed and liquefied so that it is difficult visually to stabilize the frames. The images in the various strata seem to react in a filmic way to forces given off by one another, crumbling, fading, dissolving, though not with direct systematicity. It is as if part of the attempt is to render visible sensations beneath the surface of appearance—tremors and rhythms otherwise inaccessible. The different bands seem to have a common force field beneath or behind them, its systolic and diastolic pulses variously calibrated in each of the registers.

Though Tschumi emphasizes the notational systems and their construction, the importance of the work does not lie just in these images; they are only necessary vehicles. The importance of the Transcripts is rather their offer of a radical alternative to the model of a general underlying or overarching architectural language that realizes its positive manifestation, expression, or thematization in a particular architectural object or event. In the Transcripts, an architectural Real is conceptualized precisely as a realm unrealized and unrealizable, a negativity, which becomes present in effect and as event only through displacement and negation—in the gaps, holes, and cracks that are the marks of architectural desire. A comparison with Rossi is again helpful. For him,

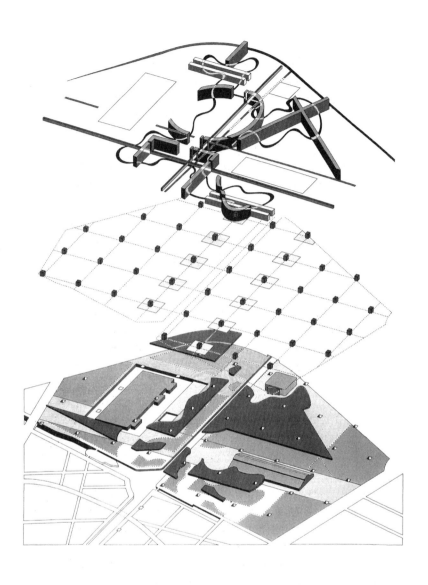

5.4
Bernard Tschumi, Parc de la Villette,
Paris, 1985, superimposition
of points, lines, and surfaces.

architecture is the historically determined mediation between an actual situation and the Symbolic order that is the social-historical city, so architecture's desire is destined for expression in an Imaginary where it remains haunted by a libidinal memory of a City it cannot fully recollect. Tschumi also links desire to a project of impossible recovery, but for him an architectural Real is the void, the excess, the emptiness produced and encircled by the symbolic systems of architecture. Architecture is the symbolic realization of the Real *and* its simultaneous negation; but the Real returns as the shock of a contingent encounter that disrupts the autonomous circulation of the symbolic apparatus. Hence the jouissance that takes the form of radical inaccessibility and difference that can be neither mediated nor superseded. Hence too the *plus-de-jouir*, the surplus or exorbitance that escapes all attempts at symbolization. The series of metonymic notations in the Transcripts registers the disjunction between the particular event of architecture and the architectural unconscious into which the actual event is constantly fading—the lost Other that architecture desires, the obscured exteriority that architecture *in effect* represents.

In the project for the Parc de la Villette (1982–1986), the attempt begun almost a decade earlier to produce the concept and the experience of architecture by blocking its actual manifestation achieves its final limit condition.[21] For the trigger that would produce architectural desire has now been assigned not to an image but to a diagrammatic grid of forty-two points superimposed by systems of orthogonal and curvilinear lines and horizontal surfaces, intersecting and meandering in a deployment of analytic elements so visually diminished and incomplete that, to eyes still trained on substance and habituated to fuller kinds of visual language, they indeed might not be counted as architecture at all. The project is more like a kind of architectural DNA: all of the information necessary for the generation and organization of a fully functioning set of programmatic-spatial events is present, but none of the substance. *La case vide*, Tschumi later called the project: the empty square, an absence, a spacing for events yet to come—not a pure architecture but an architecture of pure becoming, architecture that asserts itself as something emergent rather than final, something that we have to strain to keep in focus and, even then, hold only momentarily, just before it slips out of our perception and in the next instant is already lost.

No one understood this *maintenant* of architecture more than Jacques Derrida. What Derrida called his own *écriture double* provokes, on the one hand, an inversion of the domination of presence, which he identifies with Western metaphysics and the history of philosophy, and on the other hand enacts a new text that necessarily participates in the very principles it deconstructs, but participates as an invasion and a volatilization, releasing the dissonance of the inherited order. In his 1986 essay for the book *La Case Vide*, Derrida finds in Tschumi's project an architecture of the same formulation: *l'architecture double*, an architecture of absolute autonomy together with absolute negation, of concept and sensuous experience, an architecture that seeks to transcend form through a spacing out of form, architecture as a graph of City itself understood as a field of desire. Derrida characteristically sees all this as a play of intervals, differences, and traces of differences, as "a writing of space, a mode of spacing which makes a place for the event," or a "production of intervals without which the 'full' terms would not signify, would not function."[22] He seems to have Rossi and Eisenman in mind as comparisons when he insists that Tschumi's city, despite the absence at its heart, is not one of shadowy melancholy.

> *The* folies, *then, these* folies *in every sense [follies, madnesses]—*for once *we can say that they are not on the road to ruin, the ruin of defeat or nostalgia. They do not amount to the "absence of the work"—that fate of* mad-

ness in the classical period *of which Foucault speaks. Instead, they make up a work, they put into operation. . . . The* folies *put into operation a general dislocation; they draw into it everything that, until* maintenant, *seems to have given architecture over to meaning.*[23]

Derrida also makes the important point that among the excesses that burst through what appears to be, at first gloss, only the effacement of architecture, are parallel systems of the same sort Tschumi earlier invoked in the Manhattan Transcripts—photography, cinematography, choreography—all of which are here in the project for La Villette grafted onto the points, lines, and surfaces as hypertexts pointing beyond any actual substance to the metonymical chains of desire. Before the availability of the multimedia technology that would literally dissolve architecture into other media forms, the project for La Villette finds the multimedia conceptual apparatus that architecture produces in its own self-definition.[24] And then in 1992, Tschumi's fireworks for La Villette further offered a spectacle of performance as such, Adorno's empirical apparition, completing the dyad of trigger and effect that the essays and Advertisements first announced.

Tschumi treats the Parc de la Villette as an omnibus in which the research of Advertisements and the Manhattan Transcripts as well as the theoretical writings is amalgamated into something like a unified field theory of event space. But it is the grid of red cubes that most distinguishes La Villette. We have seen that for Eisenman the gridded collage of appropriated and repeated elements is the most adequate symbolization of the architectural Real (the grid is a perfect figure of the Symbolic). It is one of the primary characteristics of the grid superimposed on a given context that it can, on the one hand, systematically reduce the architectural raw material and perceptual data of an organizational scheme to degree zero—the point grid being understood as the

5.5
Bernard Tschumi, Parc de la Villette,
showing grid of *folies*.

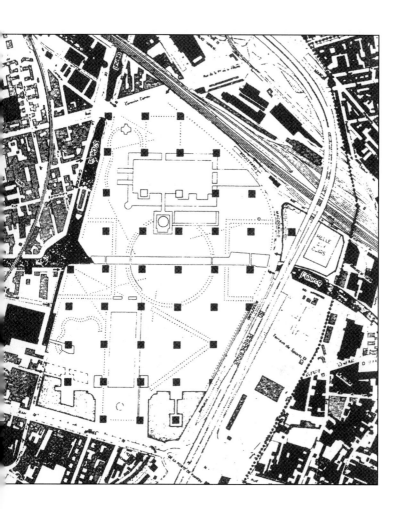

minimal limit for a work to be called architecture—and, on the other, generate a limitlessly interpretable, radically contingent, and heterogeneous set of experiences and associations. The grid announces and insists on architectural autonomy and authority, establishing as it does a different spatial order, a distinction, and a separation from the contexts in which it appears, and yet it is almost infinitely accommodating of the otherness of the fragments that it appropriates and incorporates and temporarily unites. The grid is pure relationship, with almost no form left as residue.

Around 1976–1977, in conjunction with a studio project at the Architectural Association in London, Tschumi first made use of the potential of the point grid superimposed onto an existing urban context. Joyce's Garden employs the grid as a kind of vanishing mediator, linking the random everyday events of London's Covent Garden with the textual performance of James Joyce's *Finnegans Wake*, weaving the two incommensurable systems together even as the grid itself fades into nothing and leaves only its traces and effects.[25] Tschumi very much intends the resulting heterogeneities, disjunctions, and abstractions of the project as a meditation on the then current state of mass cultural consumption and commercialism and the subject positions resulting from that condition—the same issues addressed in Advertisements, the same issues that preoccupied the Italian *architettura radicale* and in particular Archizoom's No-Stop City of 1968, which is the most direct inspiration for Tschumi's grid.[26] As for the grid itself, Archizoom used it as both enclave and global cover, local monument and endless mat. With Tschumi's development, which is finalized in La Villette, it now approaches an axiomatic in Deleuze's sense—it has no content; it is absolute relationship, even as it organizes different flows of desire.

The grid becomes a vanishing mediator, an axiomatic. The axiomatic is not an origin or a genesis; it is really the structure common to a plurality of domains, the correct concept to capture the way the grid organizes differences of architectural forms and programs. At La Villette the grid arranges points, lines, and surfaces as three "systems," which in Tschumi's vocabulary means an assemblage of spatial delineators, programmatic latencies or potentials, and subject positions related to or constructed by these two. The orthogonal lines—*cardo* and *decumanus*, the city's originating mark—are necessary for the same reason Eisenman's line from one bridge of Cannaregio to the other was necessary: to fix what would otherwise be an infinitely extending web, to specify it and modulate it to this particular site. Whereas the system of curvilinear surfaces introduces an architectural analogue to the cinematic montage that disrupts that temporary stability— "cinégramme folie," Tschumi called it: a mad orgy of events multiplied by the omnipresence of diverse media and provoking all manner of actions that can be attributed to a realm beyond necessity. One of the aims of the work is to project various planes of experience erased of functional determinants but still somehow charged (as if with a kind of performance voltage), so that an unpredictable variety of flickering functions and microperformances can be staged. "Programmatic combinations of folies: L_5: cinema-restaurant, piano bar, video theater, observatory, shops, running track, possibly small radio studio. N_5: children's folie, drawing workshop, tarzan bar, slide, water games, the administration. N_7: folie of spectacles, water wheel, first aid clinic."[27] The points, then, the *folies* themselves, are cubicled organs of intensified cultural practice, niches and cabinets corresponding to all the potential variety of social life itself.

In the Manhattan Transcripts each register or region of the work, each band, required a distinctive form and code of its own, whereas at La Villette this analytic ambition might be said to terminate in the effort to fulfill itself at the level of the molecular unit. For each point of the system, each red cube, is now further broken down, its parts permutated, substituted, and cross-referenced with all of the other cubes, until it no longer makes sense to speak of the cubes as discrete objects at all but rather of all of them together as a generic system of architectural glyphs. Typology in Rossi's sense is replaced by a hypothetically infinite combinatorial logic of frames, walls and floors, ramps, stairs, bridges, and balconies. (It is no coincidence that Tschumi chose *Finnegans Wake* for the intertext of Joyce's Garden, since *Finnegans Wake* accomplishes at the level of the word precisely what La Villette does with the architectural unit of the folly.) In place of Eisenman's unending return of the differently same, Tschumi puts into place markers of perpetual transformation. The overall effect is of a giant pulsing organism: of systolic compressions and condensations into figures and diastolic explosions into crumbling and dissolving architectural shards, creating red ripples and rhythms across La Villette's landscape.

In Derridean terms, each *folie* can be identical to itself and present as an artifact only on the condition that it is repeatable— a nonsynonymous substitution, that is, neither identical to itself nor present as such.[28] The bits and pieces of constructivism— frames with attached panels, articulated circulation devices, engineering structures and semaphores, the red color itself—which seem to give the *folies* a materiality and presence, are in fact mere semiotic residue of two like-minded searches for absolute material abstraction. Unsatisfactory as buildings, they are also essentially and necessarily vitiated as architecture—porous, impure, ghostly red things haunted by traces of failed utopias and uncertain futures. Derrida characterizes the gridded underlay of all this as the "common denominator" of the project, one without sense, "a space which in fact spaces but does not fill."[29] It is not so far from Derrida's observations to Lacan's comparison of his "unary signifier"—the elementary form of the signifier as pure difference that supports symbolic identification—to a zero in the position of a mathematical denominator: "In so far as the primary signifier is pure non-sense, it becomes the bearer of the infinitization of the value of the subject, not open to all meanings, but abolishing them, which is different."[30] Just as the zero in the position of denominator frees the numerator from any obligation to defer to it, so does Tschumi's asemic grid—let us now understand it as the unary signifier of architecture—free the points, lines, and surfaces for metonymic play even as it initiates the endless process of displacements and substitutions that comprises La Villette's signifying scheme.

But the value of the Lacanian spin for us here is twofold, since it also enables us to take into account the conception of new subject positions, which was one of Tschumi's explicit concerns. While generated out of the same generic architectural material, there is nevertheless a resultant mutual antagonism between each of the *folies*, which come to be seen as an ordered array of discontinuous centers, each itself internally decentered: so many mutations loosed from the laboratory of event space, momentarily caught in a gridded net. What results at the level of the subject is not just the direct renunciation of earlier rhetorics of communication (Baird's *dimension amoureuse*, Scott Brown's communicating communities, Jencks's multiple coding). The antagonism—or better, perhaps, agonistic autonomy (with Laclau and Mouffe in mind)[31]— also marks the morselized and incompatible subject positions characteristic of this time period (call it postmodernity) in which identities are internally contradictory, shift with contexts, and always overlap. Noting the formal similarity of Tschumi's *folies* with Hejduk's nine-square grid project[32] as well as his masques— his follies—we could think of *cinégramme folie* as a Hejdukian promiscuity run wild but now produced in the architectural Symbolic rather than the Imaginary—a form-figure that supports the visible without being seen, rather than, as in Hejduk, an image-figure appearing on an oneiric stage. All of which further effects the complete migration from an architecture of positive substance to a pure negativity of process and desire.

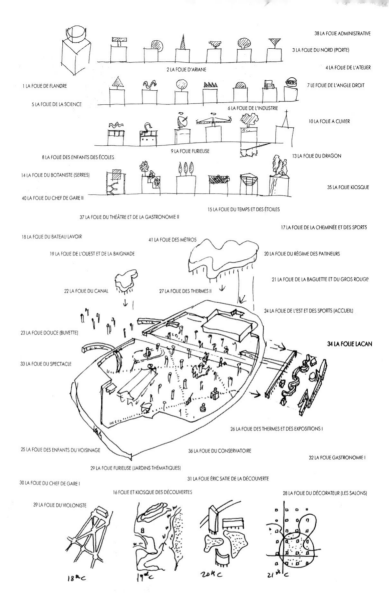

38 LA FOLIE ADMINISTRATIVE

3 LA FOLIE DU NORD (PORTE)

4 LA FOLIE DE L'ATELIER

2 LA FOLIE D'ARIANE

1 LA FOLIE DE FLANDRE

7 LE FOLIE DE L'ANGLE DROIT

5 LA FOLIE DE LA SCIENCE

6 LA FOLIE DE L'INDUSTRIE

10 LA FOLIE A CUVIER

8 LA FOLIE DES ENFANTS DES ÉCOLES

9 LA FOLIE FURIEUSE

13 LA FOLIE DU DRAGON

14 LA FOLIE DU BOTANISTE (SERRES)

40 LA FOLIE DU CHEF DE GARE II

35 LA FOLIE KIOSQUE

15 LA FOLIE DU TEMPS ET DES ÉTOILES

37 LA FOLIE DU THÉÂTRE ET DE LA GASTRONOMIE II

17 LA FOLIE DE LA CHEMINÉE ET DES SPORTS

18 LA FOLIE DU BATEAU LAVOIR

41 LA FOLIE DES MÉTROS

19 LA FOLIE DE L'OUEST ET DE LA BAIGNADE

20 LA FOLIE DU RÉGIME DES PATINEURS

21 LA FOLIE DE LA BAGUETTE ET DU GROS ROUGE

22 LA FOLIE DU CANAL

27 LA FOLIE DES THERMES II

24 LA FOLIE DE L'EST ET DES SPORTS (ACCUEIL)

23 LA FOLIE DOUCE (BUVETTE)

34 LA FOLIE LACAN

33 LA FOLIE DU SPECTACLE

26 LA FOLIE DES THERMES ET DES EXPOSITIONS I

25 LA FOLIE DES ENFANTS DU VOISINAGE

36 LA FOLIE DU CONSERVATOIRE

32 LA FOLIE GASTRONOMIE I

29 LA FOLIE FURIEUSE (JARDINS THÉMATIQUES)

30 LA FOLIE DU CHEF DE GARE I

31 LA FOLIE ÉRIC SATIE DE LA DÉCOUVERTE

16 FOLIE ET KIOSQUE DES DÉCOUVERTES

28 LA FOLIE DU DÉCORATEUR (LES SALONS)

39 LA FOLIE DU VIOLONISTE

18ᴿC   17ᴷC   20ᴷC   21ˣC

5.6

Bernard Tschumi, Parc de la Villette,
ideograms showing the permutations
of the *folies* and the grid as vanishing
mediator, 1982.

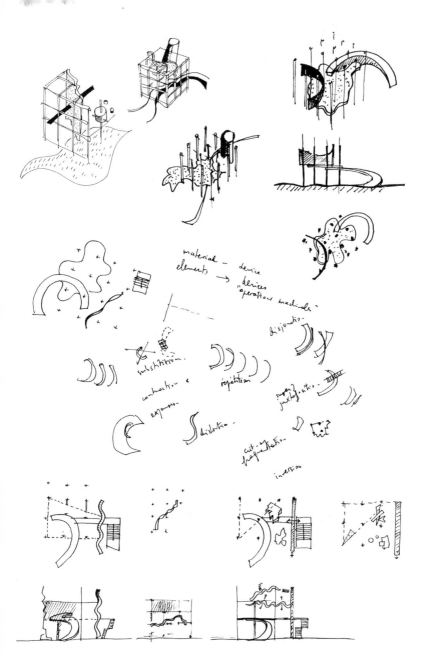

The period 1977–1978 is the moment of the late avant-garde's "discovery" of the grid as the primary signifier of architecture—trace-trait of the desiring field. And that moment of the grid operates for me as a hinge around which my entire narrative now turns and ends. For it was at that same time that Rem Koolhaas, in his study of delirious New York, found in the midst of laissez-faire development, congestion, and consumption the primary example of the schizophrenic techno-psychic machine that would preoccupy him for his entire career: the assemblage of the Downtown Athletic Club, in which the collage grid—once again in the form of the vast urban web of Manhattan—couples vertically with the skyscraper's stack of diversely functioning plateaus, themselves linked only by the technical device of an elevator—part of the "technology of the fantastic" of Coney Island—to produce previously unimaginable experiential effects out of a purely economically engineered servomechanism. "Eating oysters with boxing gloves, naked, on the 9th floor" is but one of the surrealist programmatic promises of what is, in itself, a nonarchitectural apparatus, but one whose libertine architectural potentials can be thwarted only by a failure of nerve. This grid-elevator-machine came into being through agents who refused to adopt a discourse at odds with the realities of the spasmodic "culture of congestion," refused, in fact, to adopt a discourse at all—an avant-garde without a manifesto, which must then be written retroactively.[33] Interestingly enough, in 1982–1983 the Downtown Athletic Club was rotated ninety degrees, from section into plan, to form the diagram of OMA's entry to the competition for the Parc de la Villette, which came in second place to Tschumi's.

Koolhaas's use of the grid is not simply a glorification of conventional pluralism, as with Scott Brown and Venturi, but neither is it the endlessly deferring archaeology of Eisenman or the madness of Tschumi. Rather, it is an insistence on the relationship between the randomness and contingency of experience and the presence of some architecturally inert, nondifferential, technical apparatus that nevertheless propels the differentiation of what goes on around it. The grid-elevator-machine has no substance even though it presides over all the delirious events of New York: "congestion without matter," as Koolhaas put it. What is more, there is no architectural intention behind it, only "a systematic overestimation of what exists":[34] a strange, empiricist quid pro quo in which a senseless disarray of "objectifying facts"—Manhattan's grid, the skyscraper, Coney Island—asserts itself as a set of brute things exactly where one expected to find architectural signs and representations. This is nothing less than a glimpse of the architectural Real—not Hejduk's Real seen anamorphically through the Imaginary; not Eisenman's dead still swath of symbolically constructed emptiness; and not Tschumi's disruptive, spaced-out gap of the Real. This is the intrusion of the obtuse, meaningless Thing itself, which punctures a hole in the architecture sustaining Symbolic order. The stupidity of the apparatus foregrounds the fact that the most trivial things can trigger recognitions of the anomalies in the order of the Symbolic. The obscenity of the Thing is its reminder of the fragility of that order.

In a certain sense, of course, Koolhaas simply substitutes one Name-of-the-Father for another—Wallace Harrison and Raymond Hood for Le Corbusier, Mies, and Loos—as a kind of reality test of the functionalized, instrumentalized architecture initially expelled by the late avant-garde. But in time even that little irony will melt away into a new set of "objectifying facts" whose more complete reification and mindless dispossession of the architectural subject categorically exceeds even that of the Downtown Athletic Club. Koolhaas fully understands the baleful legacy of his discovery. Take, for example, "The Ultimate Atlas for the 21st Century," in which he clinically scans the global society and economy and records thirty spaces arranged alphabetically, from "ad space" ("nothing happens until somebody sells something") to "waning space" ("delirious no more"; instead "an ecology of lawyers, dealmakers, zoning experts, and enablers grotesquely inflate the arcane complexities of 'getting things done'"), leaving the last page for an image of Le Corbusier's deserted capitol at Chandigarh, "all that's left from the Western imagination's most radical attempt to organize public space."[35] Reified negation of the primordial architectural Imaginary, the totally banal, presymbolic, economic- technological Thing that had remained in the unconscious of the late avant-garde experiment is now "retroactively" created out of the primary signifier itself.[36] Or consider Koolhaas's now classic text "Junkspace": "Junkspace exposes what previous generations kept under wraps: structures emerge like springs from a mattress, exit stairs dangle in didactic trapeze, probes thrust into space to deliver laboriously what is in fact omnipresent, free air, acres of glass hang from spidery cables, tautly stretched skins enclose flaccid non-events. . . . In Junkspace, the tables are turned: it is subsystems only, without superstructure, orphaned particles in search of framework or pattern."[37] With the evacuation of the symbolic superstructure, the architectural Other meets it demise; and when the Other collapses, we lose the subject itself— architecture.

In the negative dialectic of the late avant-garde, the object of desire that is architecture is lost from the beginning; and all mere architectural objects are attempts to fill the emptiness of that loss. Dependent on an Other, an organizing field in relation to which it is exterior and decentered, architecture is nevertheless possessed by the late avant-garde in the very form of its absence. But there was never anything to guarantee the authority or even the consistency of the Other on which architecture depends. And later, when the inert mechanical technology and economy of Koolhaas's New York has warped into the dedifferentiating economies and technologies of data management and coupled with the technocratic positivism of an architecture-managerial class, when, in other words, the necessarily excluded banality of the Thing achieves embodiment in architecture as such, then architecture will have shriveled into mere design—"purely instrumental, strictly operational," a set of opportunistic maneuvers in specific, limited contexts—possessing neither transcendence nor mystery.[38] The imperative to make do with just what is already at hand, with what is already available, is precisely what forecloses desire.

To our combinatory of categories and characteristics that describe the late avant-garde, we can now add a diachronic vector that moves from the bleached-blank mimesis of Rossi's realism through Eisenman's modernist archaeology of self-difference to the postmodern excesses and dislocations of Hejduk and Tschumi, and finally to the end altogether of a certain project of architecture.[39] This trajectory parallels (and perhaps depends on) the movement from the part-objects of Rossi's Imaginary to Eisenman's gridded Symbolic to the intrusion of the Real into the landscapes of Hejduk (where the Real interacts primarily with the Imaginary) and Tschumi (where the interaction of the Real with the Symbolic is ultimately privileged). Such is the movement of architecture's desire, traversing the limits of architectural signification; it is architecture's death drive. For it is the nature of desire that its vector twists back on itself, becoming its own object, which it can achieve only through an essential negativity—something premised on the impossibility of full satisfaction and which, as such, persists as an effect of a primordial absence. The diagram of desire is the eternal void, which is what makes signification possible and representation necessary. Thus what is glimpsed in the architecture of the late avant-garde is not the actual end of architectural practice but the real finality of its signifying network: the late avant-garde enacts architecture's inadequation to itself. The ungraspable totality of the desire called architecture inserts itself as the limit condition of all mere practices of architecture, and leaves the need for something else unassuaged.

NOTE ON THE COVER ILLUSTRATION

The cover illustration is a sketch by Aldo Rossi of a project for the Centro Direzionale competition in Turin, which Rossi and collaborators entered in 1962, and which he redrew in 1972. The sketchbook containing the drawing (along with redrawings of other early projects) is held in the Deutsches Architekturmuseum, Frankfurt. (See the exhibition catalogue Aldo Rossi, *Die Suche nach dem Glück: Frühe Zeichnungen und Entwürfe* [Munich: Prestel, 2003].)

The upper part of the drawing is a diagram of the grid of Turin, itself a trace of Turin's primordial Roman foundation. The figure below is the plan of the *centro,* imagined by Rossi in the form of a single analogical figure extruded from one module of the grid, made from the tissue of the city itself but sited on the outskirts of Turin—a "center" exteriorized, an extimate object.

The grid is the "Analogous City," architecture's *grand Autre,* which operates on the three levels of Imaginary, Symbolic, and Real; it is the object of architecture's desire. The analogous figure is one of endless possible *objets petit autre* that substitute for the never-to-be-attained Other. But there is, of course, a lack in the Other itself, a hole that Rossi attempted to fill with the letters "CD"—a cipher, meaningless in itself, which nevertheless underpins the symbolic authority of the grid. And the green patches and blue band? Do they represent the Royal Gardens and the Po River? I'm not certain; but they could be marks of the unassimilable, unimaginable Real bleeding through. —*KMH*

NOTES

DESIRE

1. See Louis Althusser, "Ideology and Ideological State Apparatuses," in *Lenin and Philosophy and Other Essays*, trans. Ben Brewster (New York: Monthly Review Press, 1971). On the autonomy problematic, see my introduction to the *Oppositions Reader: Selected Readings from a Journal of Ideas and Criticism in Architecture, 1973–1984* (New York: Princeton Architectural Press, 1998). Following Althusser, "semi-autonomy" is perhaps a better formulation, but here I will maintain the word more used in architectural discourse.

2. I intend for these claims to hold whether my analysis is of a textual concept like Rossi's typology, a single design like Eisenman's for Cannaregio, an entire career as in the case of Hejduk, or some combination of all of these, as in the case of Tschumi. I take all these together and treat them synoptically as a single project called the late avant-garde.

3. Jacques Derrida, "Structure, Sign, and Play in the Discourse of the Human Sciences," in *Writing and Difference*, trans. Alan Bass (Chicago: University of Chicago Press, 1978), pp. 278–294. I owe the appellation "Architecture in the Age of Discourse" to Anthony Vidler.

4. Manfredo Tafuri, "L'Architecture dans le Boudoir: The Language of Criticism and the Criticism of Language" (1974), in *Architecture Theory since 1968*, ed. K. Michael Hays (Cambridge: MIT Press, 1998), p. 148.

5. Ibid., p. 167.

6. Peter Bürger, *Theory of the Avant-Garde*, trans. Michael Shaw (Minneapolis: University of Minnesota Press, 1984), p. 58.

7. Colin Rowe, "Introduction," in *Five Architects* (New York: Oxford University Press, 1975), pp. 7, 8; reprinted in Hays, *Architecture Theory since 1968*.

8. Manfredo Tafuri, "Toward a Critique of Architectural Ideology" (1969), reprinted in Hays, *Architecture Theory since 1968*, p. 17.

9. Tafuri, "L'Architecture dans le Boudoir," p. 148.

10. Ibid., p. 153.

11. Denise Scott Brown, "Learning from Pop," *Casabella* 359–360 (December 1971), reprinted in Hays, *Architecture Theory since 1968*, pp. 62–64.

12. Tafuri, "L'Architecture dans le Boudoir," p. 155. Also see Massimo Scolari, "The New Architecture and the Avant-Garde," reprinted in Hays, *Architecture Theory since 1968*.

13. For a sampling of the realist discourse, see Mario Gandelsonas, "Neo-Functionalism," *Oppositions* 5 (Summer 1976): i–ii; Jorge Silvetti, "On Realism in Architecture," *Harvard Architecture Review* 1 (Spring 1980): 11–32; Martin Steinmann, "Reality as History: Notes for a Discussion of Realism in Architecture," *A+U* 69 (September 1976): 31–34; Bernard Huet, "Formalism—Realism," *L'Architecture d'Aujourd'hui* 190 (April 1977): 35–36. The last two are reprinted in Hays, *Architecture Theory since 1968*, 248–253, and 256–260, respectively.

14. Fredric Jameson, *A Singular Modernity: Essays on the Ontology of the Present* (London: Verso, 2002), pp. 198, 199.

15. Edward W. Said, *On Late Style: Music and Literature against the Grain* (New York: Pantheon, 2006), pp. 7, 8 (ellipsis in original). For Adorno's use of the concept, see Theodor W. Adorno, "Late Style in Beethoven," in *Essays on Music*, ed. Richard Leppert, trans. Susan H. Gillespie (Berkeley: University of California Press, 2002).

16. The reference is to the passage in the "culture industry" chapter in Max Horkheimer and Theodor W. Adorno, *Dialectic of Enlightenment* (New York: Continuum, 1984), p. 148: "The new ideology has as its objects the world as such. It makes use of the worship of facts by no more than elevating a disagreeable existence into the world of facts in representing it meticulously. This transference makes existence itself a substitute for meaning and right. Whatever the camera reproduces is beautiful. The disappointment of the prospect that one might be the typist who wins the world trip is matched by the disappointing appearance of the accurately photographed areas which the voyage might include. Not Italy is offered, but evidence that it exists."

17. Jacques Lacan, "The Signification of the Phallus," in *Écrits: A Selection*, trans. Alan Sheridan (New York: Norton, 1977).

18. Anika Lemaire and David Macey, *Jacques Lacan* (London: Routledge, 1977), p. 162. Lemaire quotes from Serge Leclaire, "La réalité du désir," in Centre d'etudes

Laënnec, *Sexualité humaine: Histoire, ethnologie, sociologie, psychanalyse, philosophie* (Paris: Lethielleux, 1966).

19. Is it a mere coincidence that Joseph Rykwert's *Adam's House in Paradise: The Idea of the Primitive Hut in Architectural History* was published in 1972? Or was the writing of that book driven by the same desire that drove the late avant-garde?

20. Lacan, *Écrits: A Selection*, p. 31.

21. The title of Rossi's drawing is a reference to a line in Georg Trakl's poem "Abendlied."

22. John Hejduk, *Mask of Medusa: Works, 1947–1983*, ed. Kim Shkapich (New York: Rizzoli, 1985), p. 63.

23. Fredric Jameson, "Imaginary and Symbolic in Lacan" (1977), in *The Ideologies of Theory: Essays 1971–1986*, vol. 1 (London: Routledge, 1988), p. 104.

24. Tafuri, "Toward a Critique of Architectural Ideology," p. 32.

25. Fredric Jameson, *The Political Unconscious: Narrative as a Socially Symbolic Act* (London: Routledge, 1981), p. 102. Žižek echoes Jameson: "The Lacanian Real is not some eternal essence, but strictly an historical Real. Not a Real that is simply opposed to quick historical change, but the Real that generates historical change while at the same time being reproduced by these changes." Slavoj Žižek, "Interview," *Historical Materialism* 7 (2000): 194.

26. Steven Helmling uses the concepts of deliberate and inevitable failures in *The Success and Failure of Fredric Jameson* (Albany: State University of New York Press, 2001). On the practico-inert and its counterfinality, see Jean-Paul Sartre, *Critique of Dialectical Reason* (London: Verso, 2004).

27. While I hope that each of these five chapters can be read independently, this writing has a logic that is cumulative and totalizing, which is to say that it attempts to unfold the fundamental positions in the ideological field of the late avant-garde, from which all corollary and subsequent positions derive. What is more, this introductory chapter is probably better understood if read *last* rather than first. As befitting a grappling with the negative of the sort presented here, however, I could not have told you that until now.

ANALOGY

1. Charles Jencks and George Baird, eds., *Meaning in Architecture* (New York: George Braziller, 1969).

2. As defined by Ferdinand de Saussure, *langue* (connoting "language" but also a particular "tongue") is the specific but abstract linguistic system that preexists any individual use of it and exists perfectly only within a collectivity; *parole*, the individual speech act, is the manipulation of that system to produce concrete utterances and includes localized contingencies and "accidents" like accent or personal style. See Ferdinand de Saussure, *Course in General Linguistics* (1916), ed. Charles Bally and Albert Sechehaye in collaboration with Albert Reidlinger, trans. Wade Baskin (New York: McGraw-Hill, 1959). Also see Roland Barthes *Elements of Semiology* (New York: Hill and Wang, 1968), which was the text that introduced many architecture theorists to semiotics.

3. The renewed discussion of typology was prompted by Giulio Carlo Argan, "Sul concetto di tipologia architettonica," in *Festschrift für Hans Sedlmayr*, ed. Karl Oettinger and Mohammed Rassem (Munich: C. H. Beck, 1962), translated as "On the Typology of Architecture," trans. Joseph Rykwert, *Architectural Design* 33, no. 12 (December 1963): 564–565. In the article, Argan summarizes and interprets Quatremère de Quincy's nineteenth-century theory.

4. According to Lévi-Strauss, mythemes "operate simultaneously on two levels: that of language, where they keep on having their own meaning, and that of metalanguage, where they participate as elements of a supersignification that can come only from their union." Claude Lévi-Strauss, *Structural Anthropology*, trans. Claire Jacobson and Brooke Grundfest Schoepf (New York: Basic Books, 1963), 143.

5. Theodor W. Adorno, "Functionalism Today" (1965), trans. Jane Nauman and John Smith, *Oppositions* 17 (Summer 1979): 37.

6. Jacques Lacan, "The Subversion of the Subject and the Dialectic of Desire in the Freudian Unconscious," in *Écrits: A Selection*, trans. Alan Sheridan (New York: Norton, 1977), pp. 312 ff. The reflexive structure of the query conveys the enigma of the desire of the Other, the interpellated subject's unanswerable question as to what the Other desires. "That is why the question *of* the Other, which comes back to the subject from the place from which he expects an oracular reply in some form such as 'Che vuoi?', 'What do you want?', is the one that best leads him to the path of his own desire—providing he sets out . . . to reformulate it, even without knowing it, as 'What does he want of me?'" Lacan argues that the form of the subject's question to the big Other creates a distance between the questioner and the Symbolic order and designates a crucial lack in the Symbolic. But it also

designates the moment of subjectivity. (The Italian phrase is spoken by the Devil in Jacques Cazotte, *Le diable amoureux* [1772].) Slavoj Žižek derives a theory of ideology in part from the form of this query. Žižek, "Che Vuoi?", in *The Sublime Object of Ideology* (London: Verso, 1989), pp. 87 ff.

7. Rafael Moneo, "On Typology," *Oppositions* 13 (Summer 1978): 44.

8. Aldo Rossi, *Architecture of the City* (Cambridge: MIT Press, 1982), p. 23.

9. I think it is correct to credit Rossi with the fundamental theorization of the city as the object of architecture's desire, even though Rossi would never have used that formulation. But the potential for such a notion was in the architectural discourse at least since Guy Debord's psychogeography (1955) or Roland Barthes's mythology of the Eiffel Tower (1964). Bernard Tschumi probably saw the psychic potential of the City for architecture as early as any. Mario Gandelsonas could have made a specifically structuralist-psychoanalytic theorization of the relationship by the early 1970s and did so later in "The City as the Object of Architecture," *Assemblage* 37 (December 1998).

10. Rossi, *Architecture of the City*, p. 128.

11. Rossi, cited in Tafuri, "L'Architecture dans le Boudoir," in *The Sphere and the Labyrinth: Avant-Gardes and Architecture from Piranesi to the 1970s*, trans. Pellegrino d'Acierno and Robert Connolly (Cambridge: MIT Press, 1987), p. 358.

12. I should say something here about the relation of the imagination and the Imaginary, terms that I have let slide into one another in this chapter. Lacan's optico-spatial characterization of the Imaginary is comparable to Kant's imagination at least insofar as both produce schemata that organize experience and knowledge. It is important to emphasize, however, that in contrast to Kant's "productive imagination," Lacan's Imaginary is radically unproductive, misleading the fragmented subject into thinking it is a whole. It seems right to me, in the case of Rossi's logic of types, to retain some ambiguity about the productive or unproductive imagination.

13. Aldo Rossi, *A Scientific Autobiography*, trans. Lawrence Venuti (Cambridge: MIT Press, 1981), p. 35.

14. "When I prepared this little talk for you, it was early in the morning. I could see Baltimore through the window and it was a very interesting moment because it was not quite daylight and a neon sign indicated to me every minute the change of time, and naturally there was heavy traffic and I remarked to myself that

exactly all that I could see, except for some trees in the distance, was the result of thoughts actively thinking thoughts, where the function played by the subjects was not completely obvious. In any case the so-called *Dasein* as a definition of the subject, was there in this rather intermittent or fading spectator. The best image to sum up the unconscious is Baltimore in the early morning." Jacques Lacan, "Of Structure as an Inmixing of an Otherness Prerequisite to Any Subject Whatever," in *The Languages of Criticism and the Sciences of Man*, ed. Richard Macksey and Eugenio Donato (Baltimore: Johns Hopkins University Press, 1972), p. 189.

15. Rossi, *Architecture of the City*, pp. 57–61 passim.

16. Ibid., p. 166.

17. Claude Lévi-Strauss, *The Savage Mind* (Chicago: University of Chicago Press, 1966), p. 263.

18. "Initially, no distinction was made between the typology of the house and that of the tomb. The typology of the tomb and of the sepulchral structure overlaps the typology of the house; rectilinear corridors, a central space, earth and stone materials. . . . Architecture can only use its own given elements, refusing any suggestion not born of its own making; therefore, the references to the cemetery are also found in the architecture of the cemetery, the house, and the city. Here, the monument is analogous to the relationship between life and buildings in the modern city. The cube is an abandoned or unfinished house; the cone is the chimney of a deserted factory. The analogy with death is possible only when dealing with the finished object, with the end of all things." Aldo Rossi, "The Blue of the Sky," *Oppositions* 5 (Summer 1976): 31, 34. Rossi's title is a reference to Georges Bataille's 1935 novella *Le bleu du ciel*.

19. Rossi, *Architecture of the City*, p. 174.

20. For illustrations, see *Aldo Rossi Drawings and Paintings*, ed. Morris Adjmi and Giovanni Bertolotto (New York: Princeton Architectural Press, 1993).

21. Adolf Loos, "Architektur" (1910), in *Trotzdem: 1900–1930* (Innsbruck: Brenner, 1931), pp. 109–110.

22. Rossi, *Architecture of the City*, p. 107.

23. Cited in Aldo Rossi, "An Analogical Architecture," trans. David Stewart, *Architecture and Urbanism* 56 (May 1976): 74–76.

24. Ibid., p. 74.

25. Rossi, *Architecture of the City*, p. 163.

26. Aldo Rossi, "Introduzione a Boullée," in *Scritti scelti sull'architettura e la città 1956–1972* (Milan: Città Studi, 1991), p. 360.

27. Rossi, *Architecture of the City*, pp. 40–41.

28. Rafael Moneo, "Aldo Rossi: The Idea of Architecture and the Modena Cemetery," *Oppositions* 5 (Summer 1976): 6, reprinted in *Architecture Theory since 1968*, ed. K. Michael Hays (Cambridge: MIT Press, 1998), p. 6.

29. Aldo Rossi, file 186, box 20, Rossi Papers, Getty Research Institute, cited in Mary Louise Lobsinger, "Antinomies of Realism in Postwar Italian Architecture" (PhD diss., Harvard University, 2003), p. 287.

30. Theodor W. Adorno, "On Lyric Poetry and Society," in *Notes to Literature*, ed. Rolf Tiedemann, vol. 1 (New York: Columbia University Press, 1991), pp. 38–39.

31. Moneo, "Aldo Rossi," p. 4.

32. Aldo Rossi, "Introduction," in *Aldo Rossi in America: 1976 to 1979*, ed. Kenneth Frampton (New York: Institute of Architecture and Urban Studies, 1979), p. 3.

33. Francesco Dal Co's observations are among the most acute: "'Analogous city' is the very place where monuments express mourning for the lost order to which they allude." Francesco Dal Co, "Criticism and Design," *Oppositions* 13 (Summer 1978): 10.

34. Rafael Moneo, "Postscript," in *Aldo Rossi Buildings and Projects*, ed. Peter Arnell and Ted Bickford (New York: Rizzoli, 1985), p. 314. It is helpful here to think of Roland Barthes's characterization of the *studium* of black and white photography, through which one gains access to the Symbolic, and the uninterpretable *punctum*, with its touching, tearing, bruising effect. When the *punctum* occurs, the photography will "annihilate itself as medium to be no longer a sign but the thing itself." Roland Barthes, *Camera Lucida: Reflections on Photography* (New York: Hill and Wang, 1981), p. 45.

35. Alan Colquhoun, "The Deceptions of Rationalism," paper presented at "The 1970s: The Formation of Contemporary Architectural Discourse," Graduate School of Design, Harvard University, 2001.

36. Anthony Vidler, "The Third Typology," *Oppositions* 7 (Winter 1976): 3.

37. Abstraction, for Worringer, was the most ancient form of art, which had emerged out of the desire "to divest the things of the external world of their caprice and

obscurity," to endow them with the regularity and certainty of geometry. "The urge to abstraction is the outcome of a great inner unrest inspired in man by the phenomena of the outside world. . . . We might describe this state as an immense spiritual dread of space." Wilhelm Worringer, *Abstraction and Empathy: A Contribution to the Psychology of Style*, trans. Michael Bullock (New York: International Universities Press, 1953), p. 15.

38. Peter Eisenman, "The House of the Dead as the City of Survival," in *Aldo Rossi in America*, p. 9.

39. Microanalysis embraces rather than resolves the contradictions between the conceptual demand for the new and the impossibility of its actual achievement, allowing each to pass into its other. "It is up to dialectical cognition to pursue the inadequacy of thought and thing, to experience it in the thing." Microanalysis is the form this experience takes. See Theodor W. Adorno, *Negative Dialectics*, trans. E. B. Ashton (New York: Continuum, 1973 [German ed., 1966]), p. 153.

40. Eisenman, "The House of the Dead," p. 5.

41. Ibid., p. 15.

42. Adorno, *Negative Dialectics*, p. 3.

REPETITION

1. Jacques Derrida, *Writing and Difference*, trans. Alan Bass (Chicago: University of Chicago Press, 1978), p. 5.

2. In 1971 Rossi suffered a near-fatal automobile accident, after which he became increasingly interested in the idea of architecture as a fractured body or a series of skeletal fragments to be reassembled. See Aldo Rossi, *A Scientific Autobiography* (Cambridge: MIT Press, 1984).

3. Peter Eisenman, "The Houses of Memory: The Texts of Analogy," in Aldo Rossi, *Architecture of the City* (Cambridge: MIT Press, 1982), p. 5.

4. Peter Eisenman, "The End of the Classical: The End of the Beginning, the End of the End," *Perspecta* 21 (1984): 166, reprinted in *Architecture Theory since 1968*, ed. K. Michael Hays (Cambridge: MIT Press, 1998).

5. *Cities of Artificial Excavation: The Work of Peter Eisenman, 1978–1988* (New York: Rizzoli, 1994).

6. Eisenman, "The End of the Classical," p. 172.

7. Eisenman's use of the term *competence* has two sources, I believe. One is surely Noam Chomsky, whose *Aspects of the Theory of Syntax* (Cambridge: MIT Press, 1965) Eisenman was reading at the time. But "competence" is also Clement Greenberg's word for each art medium's essential technique. I think that both meanings remain in Eisenman's use.

8. Peter Eisenman, "To Adolf Loos & Bertold Brecht," *Progressive Architecture* 55 (May 1974): 92.

9. Roland Barthes, *S/Z*, trans. Richard Miller (New York: Hill and Wang, 1974 [French ed., 1970]).

10. Eisenman's title for his introduction to the Cannaregio project, "Three Texts for Venice," is only the most convenient confirmation of the goal of this trajectory. Peter Eisenman, "Three Texts for Venice," *Domus* 611 (November 1980): 9–11.

11. Peter Eisenman, "Presentness and the Being-Only-Once of Architecture," in *Written into the Void* (New Haven: Yale University Press, 2007), p. 46. "The importance of presentness as a term for architecture is that it distinguishes [architecture as] a writing from [architecture as] an instrumentality of aesthetics and meaning" (ibid., p. 47).

12. The Name-of-the-Father is a fundamental signifier that permits signification, confers identity, and positions the subject in the Symbolic order. See Jacques Lacan, *The Seminar Book III: The Psychoses, 1955–1956*, ed. Jacques-Alain Miller, trans. Russell Grigg (New York: Norton, 1993).

13. Bernard Tschumi, "Episodes of Geometry and Lust," *Architectural Design* (January 1981), reprinted in *Questions of Space* (London: Architectural Association, 1990), p. 43.

14. W. J. T. Mitchell, *What Do Pictures Want? The Lives and Loves of Images* (Chicago: University of Chicago Press, 2005), p. 59.

15. Jacques Derrida, "Limited Inc a b c . . . ," in *Limited Inc.*, ed. Gerald Graff, trans. Jeffrey Mehlman and Samuel Weber (Evanston: Northwestern University Press, 1988).

16. Derrida offers grafting as a way of thinking about texts that combines graphic operations with processes of insertion and proliferation. Jacques Derrida, "The Double Session" (1970), in *Dissemination*, trans. Barbara Johnson (Chicago: University of Chicago Press, 1981). On the supplement, see Jacques Derrida, *Of*

Grammatology, trans. Gayatri Chakravorty Spivak (Baltimore: Johns Hopkins University Press, 1976).

17. Walter Benjamin, *The Origin of German Tragic Drama*, trans. John Osborne (London: Verso, 1998), p. 178.

18. Ibid.

19. Ibid., p. 233 (translation modified); see Benjamin, *Gesammelte Schriften*, vol. 1 (Frankfurt am Main: Suhrkamp, 1972–1989), p. 406.

20. Walter Benjamin, "Zentralpark," in *Gesammelte Schriften*, vol. 1, p. 660.

21. Ibid., p. 681.

22. Eisenman, "Three Texts for Venice," p. 9.

23. Benjamin himself appropriated this passage from Edmond Jaloux (1921) and cited it in *Gesammelte Schriften*, vol. 5, p. 366.

24. Peter Eisenman, "The End of the Classical," p. 159.

25. Ibid., p. 170.

26. Lacan emphasized the autonomy of the Symbolic order. See Jacques Lacan, *Seminar II, The Ego in Freud's Theory and in the Technique of Psychoanalysis 1954–1955*, ed. Jacques-Alain Miller, trans. Sylvana Tomaselli (New York: Norton, 1991), pp. 35, 37.

27. Peter Eisenman, "Berlin: Submission to the Restricted International Competition," *Architectural Design* 53 (January–February 1983): 92 (italics in original).

28. Perhaps it will be helpful to keep in mind that by 1986, with the re-presentation of the Verona project as *Moving Arrows, Eros, and Other Errors*, Eisenman had taken this triadic structure to the stage of reconsidering not only new forms of presentation of architectural concepts (the variously scaled and coordinated grids are now represented not in conventional architectural drawings but in a Plexiglas box of loose acetate sheets that can be randomly rearranged by the reader), but also new forms of distribution in a commercially mass-produced object with an ironically mass-produced signature on its cover, thus polemically collapsing the spaces of architectural production, architectural publication, and art commodity production. Peter Eisenman, *Moving Arrows, Eros and Other Errors: An Architecture of Absence* (London: Architectural Association, 1986).

29. Benjamin H. D. Buchloh, "Conceptual Art 1962–1969: From the Aesthetic of Administration to the Critique of Institutions," *October* 55 (Winter 1990): 111.

30. Brecht used the term *Gestus* to signify bodily gesture as opposed to spoken word. Eventually it came to be understood as the total process, the assemblage of all performative techniques into a single image.

31. Roland Barthes, *The Pleasure of the Text*, trans. Richard Miller (New York: Hill and Wang, 1975 [French ed., 1973]), p. 14. Lacan makes the pleasure/jouissance distinction in Jacques Lacan, *The Seminar Book VII: The Ethics of Psychoanalysis, 1959–1960*, ed. Jacques-Alain Miller, trans. Dennis Porter (New York: Norton, 1992).

32. For Lacan, following Freud's "Beyond the Pleasure Principle," absolute jouissance is possible only in death. The link between jouissance and the death drive is most evident Lacan's treatment of Freud's mention of *das Ding*, the Thing, which names an emptiness at the center of the Real, a black hole condensing the properties of everything existing outside of the signified. See Lacan, *The Seminar Book VII: The Ethics of Psychoanalysis*, p. 121.

33. Sigmund Freud, "Beyond the Pleasure Principle," in *The Standard Edition of the Complete Psychological Works of Sigmund Freud*, ed. James Strachey (London: Ho-garth Press, 1953–1974), vol. 18, p. 36.

34. Ibid., p. 38. It will be understood that to interpret the death drive as a wish for actual physical mortality is a misconception. Desire necessarily emerges in a "bound" state, invested in a system of signs: what Freud called a *Vorstellungs-repräsentanz*, or a conceptual representative, a structure of signification.

35. In his early work, Lacan situates the death drive in the Imaginary, describing it as a nostalgia for lost harmony and a desire to return to the pre-oedipal connection with the mother (one thinks of Rossi's yearning for the Other). In the seminars of 1954–1955, however, Lacan argues that the death drive is the fundamental tendency of the Symbolic order to produce repetition. This shifts Freud's biological model to a firmly cultural one, which is the model I have followed here. Lacan, *Seminar II*, p. 326.

36. The structural affinity of this Freudian machine to Eisenman's own negative originology is registered by critics like Rosalind Krauss, Kenneth Frampton, and Anthony Vidler, who have perceived in his work not only a preoccupation with death but also the figure of the uncanny. For the feeling of the uncanny is generated precisely in the *becoming aware* of the repetition compulsion. "It must be explained that we are able to postulate the principle of a repetition-compulsion

in the unconscious mind, based upon instinctual activity and probably inherent in the very nature of the instincts—a principle powerful enough to overrule the pleasure-principle. . . . Taken in all, the foregoing prepares us for the discovery that whatever reminds us of this inner repetition-compulsion is perceived as uncanny." Freud, *Standard Edition*, vol. 17, p. 238.

37. Peter Eisenman, "Introduction," in *Aldo Rossi in America: 1976 to 1979*, ed. Kenneth Frampton (New York: Institute of Architecture and Urban Studies, 1979), p. 3 (my emphasis).

38. Roland Barthes has observed that "the greatest modernist works linger as long as possible, in a sort of miraculous stasis, on the threshold of Literature itself, in this anticipatory situation in which the density of life is given and developed without yet being destroyed through its consecration as an [institutionalized] sign system." Roland Barthes, *Writing Degree Zero* (New York: Hill and Wang, 1968), p. 39.

39. Lacan, *Seminar II*, p. 219.

ENCOUNTER

1. Jacques Lacan, *The Seminar Book VII: The Ethics of Psychoanalysis 1959–1960*, ed. Jacques-Alain Miller, trans. Dennis Porter (New York: Norton, 1992), p. 282.

2. John Hejduk, *Mask of Medusa: Works, 1947–1983*, ed. Kim Shkapich (New York: Rizzoli, 1985), p. 50.

3. John Hejduk, *Práce* [Practice] (Prague: OBEC ArchitektD, 1991), p. 33.

4. "In painting, the English term still life and the Italian term *natura morta* haunt. Not an innocent combining of two words in English, 'still life,' in Italian 'dead nature.' If the painter could, by a single transformation, take a three-dimensional still life and paint it on a canvas into a *natura morta*, could it be possible for the architect to take the natura morta of a painting and, by a single transformation, build it into a still life?" John Hejduk, *Adjusting Foundations*, ed. Kim Shkapich (New York: Monacelli Press, 1995), p. 48. It is useful to compare Hejduk's still life projects with Aldo Rossi's domestic landscapes.

5. Hejduk, *Mask of Medusa*, p. 67.

6. The early work of Hejduk and Eisenman was presented together in *Five Architects* (New York: Oxford University Press, 1972).

7. Cited in Carol Armstrong and Laura Giles, *Cézanne in Focus: Watercolors from the Henry Rose and Pearlman Collection* (Princeton: Princeton University Art Museum, 2002), p. 80.

8. Hejduk, *Mask of Medusa*, pp. 62, 50, 62.

9. Walter Benjamin, "On Some Motifs in Baudelaire," in *Illuminations*, ed. Hannah Arendt, trans. Harry Zohn (New York: Schocken Books, 1977), p. 188. The invocation of Marcel Proust's notion of involuntary memory signals a kind of memory that seizes the viewer suddenly and unexpectedly, reminding him of a previous experience, but with an affective intensity unavailable to willfully revived memories.

10. Jacques Lacan, *The Four Fundamental Concepts of Psycho-Analysis*, trans. Alan Sheridan (New York: Norton, 1978), p. 107.

11. "On one side of the wall (the past), the circulatory elements—ramp, stair, elevator—were placed. They were volumetric, opaque, monochromatic, in perspective with the structure grounded. The color was white, grey, black; the materials reinforced concrete, steel and cement. Once the single inhabitant passed through the wall he was in a space overlooking a landscape (trees? Water? Earth? Sky?) which was basically private, contemplative and reflective. There were three suspended floors cantilevered from the collective elements. The materials on this side of the wall were glass and reflective metal; a fluidity was sought after. Whereas the collective side was hard, tough, concrete, the private side was inwardly reflective, a light shattering into fragments, mirror images moving along the polished surfaces of metal." Hejduk, *Mask of Medusa*, p. 59.

12. John Hejduk, *Victims* (London: Architectural Association, 1986).

13. *Aldo Rossi, John Hejduk* (Zurich: Arbeitsberichte der Architekturabteilung, 1973). The catalog is introduced with a German translation of Colin Rowe's introduction to *Five Architects*.

14. Daniele Vitale, "Inventions, Translations, Analogies: Projects and Fragments by Aldo Rossi," *Lotus International* 25 (1979): 55.

15. Hejduk, *Mask of Medusa*, p. 136. The project was, in part, a response to the call by the organizers of the 1975 Venice Biennale to bring awareness to the degraded state of the Giudecca and the Mulino Stucky and "to bring them back to life." See Carlo Ripa di Meana and Christian Boltanski, *A proposito del Mulino*

Stucky: Environmedia, partecipazioni libere (A Propos of Mulino Stucky: Environ-media, Free Contributions) (Venice: Alfieri, 1975), p. 5. The Mulino Stucky was a pasta mill at the western end of the Giudecca designed by Ernest Wullkopf in the late nineteenth century. It was closed in 1954 and was in ruin when Hejduk made his proposal. This is the full description of the project: "The Mulino Stucky Building's exteriors are painted black. The Mulino Stucky Building's interiors are painted white. The long, extended walls of the Cemetery for the Ashes of Thought are black on one side and white on the other side. The top and end surfaces of the long extended walls are grey. Within the walls are one foot square holes at eye level. Within each one foot square hole is placed a transparent cube containing ashes. Under each hole upon the wall there is a small bronze plaque indicating the title, and only the title of a work, such as Remembrance of Things Past, The Counterfeiters, The Inferno, Paradise Lost, Moby Dick, etc. Upon the exterior of the walls of the Mulino Stucky Building are small plaques with the names of the authors of the works: Proust, Gide, Dante, Milton, Melville, etc. In the lagoon on a man-made island is a small house for the sole habitation of one individual for a limited period of time. Only one individual for a set period of time may inhabit the house, no others will be permitted to stay on the island during its occupation. The lone individual looks across the lagoon to the Cemetery for the Ashes of Thought." Reprinted in Hejduk, *Mask of Medusa*, p. 80.

16. Hejduk, *Mask of Medusa*, p. 85. "What I am doing is I am the questionnaire upon the question. I am the interrogation upon the interrogator. So when Rossi and all those things in Europe are going on, the totalitarian stuff which has to do with deep political and social meanings, then I answer it with The Cemetery for the Ashes of Thought. People did see that, but baby, nobody talks about that project. The Cemetery for the Ashes of Thought was one man's confrontation with that whole European condition." Ibid., p. 130.

17. Lacan, *The Seminar Book VII: The Ethics of Psychoanalysis*, p. 121. This is the passage from Heidegger: "When we fill the jug, the pouring that fills it flows into the empty jug. The emptiness, the void, is what does the vessel's holding. The empty space, this nothing of the jug, is what the jug is as the holding vessel. . . . But if the holding is done by the jug's void, then the potter who forms sides and

bottom on his wheel does not, strictly speaking, make the jug. He only shapes the clay. No—he shapes the void. . . . The vessel's thingness does not lie at all in the material of which it consists, but in the void that holds. Martin Heidegger, "The Thing," in *Poetry, Language, Thought*, trans. A. Hofstadter (New York: Harper and Row, 1971), p. 169.

18. In Seminar VII, Lacan claims that art as such is always organized around the central void of the impossible-real Thing, and mentions in particular the functioning of the void in the visual arts and in architecture.

19. Freud, "Project for a Scientific Psychology," in *The Standard Edition of the Complete Psychological Works of Sigmund Freud*, ed. James Strachey (London: Hogarth Press, 1953–1974), vol. 1, p. 331.

20. Lacan, *The Seminar Book VII: The Ethics of Psychoanalysis*, p. 71.

21. Ibid., p. 140.

22. Ibid., pp. 71, 58.

23. Hejduk, *Mask of Medusa*, p. 83.

24. See Jacques-Alain Miller, "Extimité," in *Lacanian Theory of Discourse: Subject, Structure, and Society*, ed. Mark Bracher et al. (New York: New York University Press, 1994). Lacan uses the term infrequently, but it is elaborated by Miller "to designate in a problematic manner the real in the symbolic" (p. 75). "Extimacy says that the intimate is Other" (p. 76).

25. Ray Bradbury, *The Machineries of Joy* (New York: Simon and Schuster, 1964), p. 53, cited in Gilles Deleuze and Felix Guattari, *A Thousand Plateaus* (Minneapolis: University of Minnesota Press, 1987), p. 262.

26. M. M. Bakhtin, *Rabelais and His World*, trans. Helene Iswolsky (Cambridge: MIT Press, 1968), p. 317.

27. Hejduk, *Mask of Medusa*, p. 39.

28. Jean-Paul Sartre, *Being and Nothingness: An Essay on Phenomenological Ontology*, trans. Hazel E. Barnes (London: Methuen, 1957), p. 288. Lacan's own interest in Christianity followed from the vocation it shared with psychoanalysis to deal with what can never be fully known.

29. "John Hejduk or, The Architect Who Drew Angels," conversation with David Shapiro, *Architecture and Urbanism*, no. 244 (1991): 61.

30. For a discussion of Hejduk's work as a peculiarly American quest for a promised land, see Catherine Ingraham, "Errand, Detour, and the Wilderness Urbanism of John Hejduk," in *Hejduk's Chronotope*, ed. K. Michael Hays (New York: Princeton Architectural Press, 1996), pp. 129–142.

31. The entire suite of thirty-two Enclosures is published in K. Michael Hays, *Sanctuaries: The Last Works of John Hejduk* (New York: Whitney Museum, 2003).

32. Le Corbusier, *Oeuvre complète 1946–52* (Zurich: Girsberger, 1953), p. 88.

33. Gilles Deleuze and Felix Guattari, "Year Zero: Faciality," in *A Thousand Plateaus*, p. 115.

34. Ibid., p. 167. Deleuze and Guattari build on and "correct" Lacan and Sartre in terms of the gaze. "The gaze is but secondary in relation to the gazeless eyes, to the black hole of faciality. The mirror is but secondary in relation to the white wall of faciality" (p. 171).

SPACING

1. Bernard Tschumi, "The Pleasure of Architecture," in *Questions of Space: Lectures on Architecture* (London: AA Publications, 1990), p. 55.

2. Bernard Tschumi, *Architecture and Disjunction* (Cambridge: MIT Press, 1994). There are few serious treatments of Tschumi's early work. The best remains Louis Martin, "Transpositions: On the Intellectual Origins of Tschumi's Architectural Theory," *Assemblage*, no. 11 (April 1990).

3. Bernard Tschumi, "Questions of Space: The Pyramid and the Labyrinth (or the Architectural Paradox)," *Studio International*, September-October 1975, p. 138. The essay was published in a slightly different form as "The Architectural Paradox," in *Architecture and Disjunction*.

4. Ibid., p. 138.

5. Theodor Adorno, "Functionalism Today" (1965), trans. Jane Nauman and John Smith, *Oppositions* 17 (Summer 1979): 37.

6. Tschumi, "Questions of Space," p. 142.

7. Ibid., pp. 141, 138.

8. Ibid., p. 142. Adorno writes, "The phenomenon of fireworks is prototypical for artworks. . . . Fireworks are apparitions [par excellence]: they appear empirically yet are liberated from the burden of the empirical, which is the obligation for duration; they are a sign from heaven yet artifactual, an ominous warning, a script

that flashes up, vanishes, and indeed cannot be read for its meaning." Theodor W. Adorno, *Aesthetic Theory*, trans. Robert Hullot-Kentor (Minneapolis: University of Minnesota Press, 1997), p. 107.

9. Tschumi, "Questions of Space," p. 142.

10. Jacques Lacan, *Écrits: A Selection*, trans. Alan Sheridan (New York: Norton, 1977), p. 319.

11. Bernard Tschumi, "Architecture and Transgression," in *Architecture and Disjunction*, p. 73. Originally published in *Oppositions* 7 (Winter 1976). For one of the few accounts of Advertisements, see Kari Jormakka, "The Most Architectural Thing," in *Surrealism and Architecture*, ed. Thomas Mical (London: Routledge, 2005).

12. Tschumi, "Architecture and Transgression," p. 76.

13. Ibid., p. 94.

14. It is interesting to note that in Lacan's reading of the Antigone story in Seminar VII, the key term is *Ate,* normally meaning fate or doom but which he renders as "transgression." Antigone transgresses Creon's laws and faces death in a way adequate to her desire.

15. "Something on the order of a *subject* can be discerned on the recording surface. It is a strange subject, however, with no fixed identity, wandering about over the body without organs, but always remaining peripheral to the desiring-machines, being defined by the share of the product it takes for itself, garnering here, there, and everywhere a reward, in the form of a becoming or an avatar, being born of the states that it consumes and being reborn with each new state. 'It's me, and so it's mine' [*c'est donc moi, c'est donc à moi*]. . . . The subject is produced as a mere residue alongside the desiring machines." Gilles Deleuze and Félix Guattari, *Anti-Oedipus* (New York: Viking Press, 1977), pp. 17–19.

16. Bernard Tschumi, *The Manhattan Transcripts: Theoretical Projects* (New York: Academy Editions, 1981), p. xxviii.

17. Georges Bataille, "The Notion of Expenditure," in *Visions of Excess: Selected Writings, 1927–1939* (Minneapolis: University of Minnesota Press, 1985), p. 118.

18. The program for the Transcripts is based on "the most common formula plot: the archetype of murder." Tschumi, *The Manhattan Transcripts*, p. 7. In archetypal terms, murder is the interface between nature and culture, the founding violence that sets in motion the entire symbolic economy.

19. In this regard, on the topic of reification, it is as if Tschumi plays Debord against Rossi's Lukács and Eisenman's Adorno.

20. *Tschumi on Architecture: Conversations with Enrique Walker* (New York: Monacelli Press, 2006), p. 34.

21. The competition was held in 1982–1983; Tschumi was awarded the project in 1983. Later came the publications *La Case Vide: La Villette, 1985* (London: Architectural Association, 1986), and *Cinégramme Folie: Le Parc de la Villette* (Princeton: Princeton Architectural Press, 1987), both of which should be understood not as mere records of the project but as further instantiations of it.

22. Jacques Derrida, *Positions*, trans. Alan Bass (Chicago: University of Chicago Press, 1981), p. 27.

23. Jacques Derrida, "Point de folie—Maintenant l'architecture," trans. Kate Linker, in *La Case Vide*, p. 7.

24. Tschumi is quite explicit about this in a 1988 lecture on La Villette published as "De-. Dis-. Ex-," in *Remaking History*, ed. Barbara Kruger and Phil Mariani (Seattle: Bay Press for Dia Art Foundation, 1989).

25. Is it just a fascinating coincidence that, at the very end of his career in 1975–1976, Lacan gave a seminar on James Joyce, under the title *Le sinthome*? The seminar extends the Real-Symbolic-Imaginary triad, adding a fourth component, the sinthome (an old French spelling of *symptom*), as that which holds together the knot of the triad constantly threatening to come undone (thereby supplementing the stabilizing and nominating functions of the Name-of-the-Father). The rupture that the sinthome indexes is most apparent in the art of writing, particularly in Joyce's *Finnegans Wake*.

26. Tschumi's recollection of the importance of Archizoom: "I was fascinated by the images and the subtext of Archizoom and had invited them to the AA. Even today, I think *No-Stop City* is one of the strokes of genius of that period and definitely one of the most important projects of the second half of the twentieth century. *No-Stop City* shed light on how an architectural activity could be critical, how one could develop critical thinking by means of a project, as opposed to a written article—with the same, or more effect. It was an ironic statement of extraordinary architectural intelligence, which acknowledged that as an intellectual, one cannot change the system, only verify it and show where it is going. It also means that,

paradoxically, one may find oneself one day in the situation of actually building one's verification." *Tschumi on Architecture*, p. 19.

27. *Cinégramme Folie*, p. 27.

28. "It is because of *différance* that the movement of signification is possible only if each so-called 'present' element, each element appearing on the scene of presence, is related to something other than itself, thereby keeping within itself the mark of the past element, and already letting itself be vitiated by the mark of its relation to the future element, this trace being related no less to what is called the future than to what is called the past, and constituting what is called the present by means of this very relation to what it is not: what it absolutely is not, not even a past or a future as a modified present. An interval must separate the present from what it is not in order for the present to be itself. . . . In constituting itself, in dividing itself dynamically, this interval is what might be called *spacing*, the becoming-space of time or the becoming-time of space *(temporization)*. Jacques Derrida, "Difference" (1972), in *Margins of Philosophy*, trans. Alan Bass (Chicago: University of Chicago Press, 1982), p. 13.

29. Derrida, "Point de folie," p. 7.

30. Jacques Lacan, *The Four Fundamental Concepts of Psycho-Analysis*, trans. Alan Sheridan (New York: Norton, 1978), p. 252.

31. Ernesto Laclau and Chantal Mouffe, *Hegemony and Socialist Strategy* (London: Verso, 1985).

32. The so-called nine-square problem—a grid of three by three squares used to investigate the purely formal relationship between center and periphery, plane and volume, grid and insertions—led to Hejduk's Texas House series (1954–1963) and is related to Peter Eisenman's first house projects. The nine-square problem was a foundational project in design studios at Cooper Union. See John Hejduk, *Mask of Medusa: Works, 1947–1983*, ed. Kim Shkapich (New York: Rizzoli, 1985), pp. 37–38.

33. Rem Koolhaas, *Delirious New York: A Retroactive Manifesto* (New York: Oxford University Press, 1978).

34. Rem Koolhaas et al., *Small, Medium, Large, Extra-large* (New York: Monacelli, 1995), p. 51.

35. Rem Koolhaas, "The Ultimate Atlas for the 21st Century," *Wired* (June 2003): 169.

36. This economic-technological Thing is only a specific instance of a more general relationship to the Thing that is capital. As Žižek has suggested, "Today more than ever, capital is the Thing *par excellence*: a chimeric apparition which, although it can no where be spotted as a positive, clearly delimited entity, nevertheless functions as the ultimate Thing regulating our lives." Slavoj Žižek, *Enjoy Your Symptom: Jacques Lacan in Hollywood and Out* (London: Routledge, 2001), pp. 122–123.

37. Rem Koolhaas, "Junkspace," in Chuihua Judy Chung, Jeffrey Inaba, et al., eds., *Harvard Design School Guide to Shopping* (Cologne: Taschen, 2001).

38. The value of this evolution is, of course, more ambiguous than I have put it here. Consider Sanford Kwinter's assertion that "architecture has begun to vanish as a discipline, and some of us are not mourning. More and more, we like to think of practice in far more generic and elastic terms, we think of what we do as *design*, and like the generations before us, we feel the need for an escape velocity that might carry us beyond the sclerosis of inherited boundaries." Sanford Kwinter, "Leap in the Void: A New Organon?" in *Anyhow* (Cambridge: MIT Press, 1998), p. 24. It is interesting in this context to be reminded of Koolhaas's reaction to this manifesto launched by Sanford Kwinter and joined by Alejandro Zaera-Polo, Ben van Berkel, and Greg Lynn during the 1997 Anyhow conference in Rotterdam: "They had fresh and new ambitions and postures—antisemantic, purely operational—represented in virtuoso computer (in)animation. . . . I remember being critical of their claim, then, that they had gone beyond form to sheer performance, and their claim that they had gone beyond the semantic in to the purely instrumental and strictly operation. What I find (still) baffling is their hostility to the semantic. Semiotics is more triumphant than ever—as evidenced, for example, in the corporate world or branding—and the semantic critique may be more useful than ever. . . . It seems a potential tragedy that, once again, architectural discourse is hostile to a phenomenon at the moment of its greatest use." Rem Koolhaas, "Spot Check: A Conversation between Rem Koolhaas and Sarah Whiting," *Assemblage* 40 (December 1999): 46.

39. The suggestion here is that the category of late avant-garde holds within itself at a smaller scale its own moments of realism, modernism, and postmodernism.